PRENTICE-HALL FOUNDATIONS OF FINANCE SERIES

PRENTICE-HALL FOUNDATIONS OF FINANCE SERIES

Ezra Solomon, *Editor*

Capital Markets and Institutions

Second Edition

Herbert E. Dougall

C. O. G. Miller Professor of Finance, Emeritus
Stanford University

PRENTICE-HALL, INC., Englewood Cliffs, New Jersey

P 13–113621–6
C 13–113639–9

Library of Congress Catalog Card No. 77–108322
Printed in the United States of America

Current printing (last digit):
10 9 8 7 6 5 4 3 2 1

PRENTICE-HALL INTERNATIONAL, INC., *London*
PRENTICE-HALL OF AUSTRALIA, PTY. LTD., *Sydney*
PRENTICE-HALL OF CANADA, LTD., *Toronto*
PRENTICE-HALL OF INDIA PRIVATE LIMITED, *New Delhi*
PRENTICE-HALL OF JAPAN, INC., *Tokyo*

Editor's Note

The subject matter of financial management is in the process of rapid change. A growing analytical content, virtually nonexistent ten years ago, has displaced the earlier descriptive treatment as the center of emphasis in the field.

These developments have created problems for both teachers and students. On the one hand, recent and current thinking, which is addressed to basic questions that cut across traditional divisions of the subject matter, do not fit neatly into the older structure of academic courses and texts in corporate finance. On the other hand, the new developments have not yet stabilized and as a result have not yet reached the degree of certainty, lucidity, and freedom from controversy that would permit all of them to be captured within a single, straightforward treatment at the textbook level. Indeed, given the present rate of change, it will be years before such a development can be expected.

One solution to the problem, which the present Foundations of Finance Series tries to provide, is to cover the major components of the subject through short independent studies. These individual essays provide a vehicle through which the writer can concentrate on a single sequence of ideas and thus communicate some of the excitement of current thinking and controversy. For the teacher and student, the separate self-contained books provide a flexible up-to-date survey of current thinking on each subarea covered and at the same time permit maximum flexibility in course and curriculum design.

EZRA SOLOMON

Preface

The aim of the second edition is the same as that of the first—to present a careful but uncomplicated study of the institutions through which long-term funds are funnelled into the several markets, and of the demand for funds in the markets, so that the resulting yields can be noted and analysed. The data are again integrated in a master table for the capital market as a whole.

The dramatic changes in the capital markets and in the investment policies of major financial institutions since 1965 have required a very thorough revision of the book. The forces lying behind the "credit crunch" of 1966, the rise in yields on fixed-income instruments to unprecedented heights, and the second "crunch" in 1969 are described and measured. All data have been updated through 1968 and, together with partial information for 1969, form the basis for appropriate comment. The references include a number of recent works.

Although the data have been drawn from primary sources wherever possible, the task of developing flow-of-funds figures has again been eased by use of information compiled by Bankers Trust Company in its *Investment Outlook*. Permission of the Company to cite this source is gratefully acknowledged.

The author is indebted for many ideas and much information to a number of persons and organizations, and for data in advance of publication from the National Association of Mutual Savings Banks, the Federal Deposit Insurance Corporation, the United States Savings and Loan League, the Institute of Life Insurance, and the Securities and Exchange Commission.

H.E.D.

Table of Contents

Tables

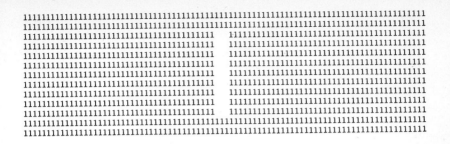

Nature and Scope of the
Capital Markets

Economic Capital

THE economic strength of a nation may be measured by the value of its accumulated wealth and by the rate at which it grows through savings and investment. National wealth includes all structures, equipment, inventories, land, monetary metals, and net foreign assets. The total of these components in the United States was estimated at $2,828 billions at the end of 1967. The first three, which we can label capital goods, totaled $2,305 billions.[1] This aggregate of economic capital (less $325 billions representing consumers' durable equipment) had been built up by the allocation of income to investment for future production rather than to current consumption.

In the strict economic sense, *capital* means capital goods, or the stock of means of production: buildings, equipment, and inventories.[2] Economic capital does not include claims to assets; it consists of the

---

[1] J. W. Kendrick and others, "The Wealth of the United States," *Finance: The Magazine of Money* (January 1967), pp. 12–13; U.S. Department of Commerce, *Statistical Abstract of the United States: 1968* (89th ed.), Washington, D.C.: U.S. Government Printing Office, 1968, p. 336.

[2] The traditional distinction between land (natural resources) and capital becomes less apparent as the use of land becomes progressively commercialized.

assets themselves. Consumer durable goods such as passenger automobiles are excluded because they yield immediate satisfactions. However, somewhat arbitrarily, residential dwellings are included, not only because of their great value but also because housing can be thought to produce a service.

Capital goods owned by individuals consist mainly of residential housing; by businesses, of fixed assets and inventories; and by government, of publicly owned facilities. For our purpose, governments, like business firms, should be viewed as producers needing financing rather than as ultimate consumers, even though they do not operate for the economic market as businesses do. Governments owned about $390 billions of the $2,300 billions of economic capital in 1967.[3]

Capital Formation

Capital formation is the growth in the stock of economic capital goods. It is measured in dollars and in relation to Gross National Product (GNP). Annual domestic investment is stated as either gross or net. Net private capital formation is the addition to the stock of capital goods less depreciation of those goods already on hand. The substantial increase in the stock of private domestic capital, both gross and net, for selected years since World War II, is indicated in Table 1-1, together with Gross National Product and the rate of gross growth in terms of GNP. Because it is the gross investment that must be financed, mainly in the capital markets, our main interest lies in that figure.

Table 1-1.   Private Domestic Capital Formation in the United States, 1950–1968, Billions of Dollars

	1950	1955	1960	1965	1968
Producers' durable equipment	$ 18.7	$ 23.8	$ 30.3	$ 45.8	$ 60.8
New construction (other than residential structures)	9.2	14.3	18.1	25.5	29.2
Business inventories	6.8	6.0	3.6	9.6	7.7
Residential structures	19.4	23.3	22.8	27.2	29.9
Total· gross	$ 54.1	$ 67.4	$ 74.8	$108.1	$127.6
Capital consumption allowances	18.3	31.5	43.4	59.8	74.3
Total net	$ 35.8	$ 35.9	$ 31.4	$ 48.3	$ 53.3
Gross National Product	$284.8	$398.0	$503.8	$684.9	$860.6
Rate of gross capital formation, per cent	19.0	17.0	14.8	15.8	14.8

Sources: U.S. Department of Commerce, *Statistical Abstract of the United States* and *Survey of Current Business.*

[3]Estimated for 1967 from data in Kendrick and others, "The Wealth of the United States." Capital goods in the hands of governments are not included in the Department of Commerce estimates shown in Table 1-1. Governments are treated as consumers, possibly because of the difficulty of estimating the amount of government capital.

In measuring present and estimated future capital growth, attention often centers on business plant and equipment expenditures. Two major series of this limited concept of capital formation are in wide use. The first consists of the first two figures in Table 1-1, which amounted to $90 billions in 1968, or 10.5 per cent of GNP. The Council of Economic Advisers has suggested that achieving a growth of output of 4 per cent per year requires "private investment" to be between 10 and 11 per cent of GNP.[4] An even more widely used figure of business plant expenditures is reported by the Securities and Exchange Commission and by the Office of Business Economics of the Department of Commerce, and advance quarterly estimates are published in the *Survey of Current Business*. This figure was projected at an annual rate of $77 billions for 1970. It excludes investment by farmers, professionals, institutions, real estate firms, and insurance companies.

Capital Formation and the Capital Markets

In primitive societies the savers and users of capital were largely the same, although some exchange of capital goods for consumer goods occurred through barter. There was no financing problem. But in a modern capitalistic economy instruments representing money and claims to money are necessary for specialization and the division of labor and for the transfer of savings to those who invest in capital goods. Capital formation would be virtually impossible without money and a market. Extensive institutional machinery is necessary to channel the money value of savings generated by some units in the economy to those who use these savings. Although those who save make some direct investments—as, for example, a firm that uses profits to expand its plant— most savings are collected and redistributed through the capital markets for others to employ. The existence of these markets largely makes possible the process of capital formation. As Lavington asserts in his classic work, the great growth in the industrial power of modern communities has been accomplished by an increase in specialization, which in turn has been "dependent on the provision of means and facilities for effecting payments in general and on the provision of facilities for effecting those particular payments by which capital is transferred from the control of one party to another."[5]

There is no such thing as a market for capital, that is, the economic capital goods themselves. But there is a market, or rather a group of markets, for the dollar instruments that represent either title to or claims to capital and to the other resources owned by government,

---

[4]*Economic Report of the President*, Washington, D.C.: U.S. Government Printing Office (1963) p. 62. Actually, GNP increased about 10 per cent per year in the period 1963 through 1968, while private nonresidential investment averaged 10 per cent of GNP.

[5]F. Lavington, *The English Capital Market* (London: Methuen & Co., Ltd., 1921), pp. 2–3.

business, and individuals. Just as economic capital represents assets of a more or less permanent nature, *capital* can be used to mean the money value of the instruments of ownership and of long-term claims to assets, and *capital markets* to mean the markets in which these instruments are transferred. This usage of terms in turn suggests a distinction between the capital markets, or markets for longer-term funds, and the money market for short-term funds (obligations with a year or less to maturity).[6]

The Money Market

The money market provides facilities for the quick and dependable transfer of short-term debt instruments used to finance the needs of business, government, agriculture, and consumer. A distinction may be made between the direct, negotiated, or customers' money market and the impersonal, or open, market. The former is found wherever banks and other financial firms supply funds to local customers. It also includes the bank correspondents who funnel funds into larger centers such as New York for direct lending. The open money market is mainly the complex of facilities in New York where idle funds, drawn from all over the country, are transferred through intermediaries. Federal Reserve banks, commercial banks (especially the big "money market" banks), business corporations with idle funds, insurance companies, foreign suppliers (including foreign banks), finance companies, state and local governments, and individuals all make short-term funds available to other similar institutions, to the United States Treasury, and to securities brokers and dealers for "street" loans. The intermediaries are chiefly Federal Reserve banks, big commercial banks, and government securities dealers. The instruments representing the short-term funds are chiefly Federal funds (excess member bank reserves), short-term government securities, bankers' acceptances, and commercial paper.[7]

---

[6]Such distinctions are not made by either Lavington or Macrae in their descriptions of the English scene. Lavington uses the term *capital market* in the title but *money market* in the text. And his discussion includes both short- and long-term instruments. F. Lavington, *The English Capital Market*. Macrae emphasizes the long term but devotes considerable attention to monetary policy. Norman Macrae, *The London Capital Market* (London: Staples Press, Ltd., 1955) .

[7]Walter Bagehot's *Lombard Street* is a classic work dealing with the English money market in the sense that we use the term here. A modern edition with a new introduction is published by Richard D. Irwin, Inc. (1962). For a description of the American money market, see Marcus Nadler, Sipa Heller, and S. S. Shipman, *The Money Market and Its Institutions* (New York: The Ronald Press Company, 1955). Less thorough but informative sources are C. H. Madden, *The Money Side of the Street* (New York: Federal Reserve Bank of New York, 1959); and J. T. Madden, Marcus Nadler, and Sipa Heller, *Money Market Primer* (New York: The Ronald Press Company, 1948). Robinson devotes part of his attention to the money market. R. I. Robinson, *The Money and Capital Markets* (New York: McGraw-Hill Book Company, 1964).

The Capital Markets: General Character and Definition

Capital markets are the complex of institutions and mechanisms whereby intermediate-term funds (loans of up to 10 years maturity for example) and long-term funds (longer-maturity loans and corporate stocks) are pooled and made available to business, government, and individuals, and whereby instruments already outstanding are transferred.[8] As in the case of the money market, the capital markets are local, regional, and national in scope.

Because they deal with instruments representing longer-term funds, the capital markets involve capital in the economic sense. Funds raised through debt instruments by business and individuals are invested in fixed assets and inventories. Admittedly, the proceeds of government bonds and corporate shares are used to finance a variety of expeditures and types of assets.

The Investment Market

In the economic sense, investment means the commitment of funds to capital assets. In this sense, investors are the *users* of funds—their own or those of others acquired in the market. In the financial and popular sense, however, investors are on the other side of the transaction—they *supply* funds to business, government, and individuals by acquiring debt and equity instruments with their savings. In financial terminology then, the investment market is similar to the capital market, except that it is usually restricted to security instruments of all maturities. In this book we shall use the term *investors* in the financial sense and the term *investment market*, or *financial market*, to mean the entire market for funds.

Interrelations of the Money and Capital Markets

The money and capital markets (or group of markets) are not independent, for the following reasons:

(1) Suppliers of funds may choose to direct them to either or to both markets, depending on their investment policies and on the available rates of return.

(2) Users of funds may obtain them from either market. For example, a corporation needing funds for additional inventory may bor-

---

[8]Traditionally, the money market has been described as the market for short-term debt, with a year or less to maturity, and the capital market as dealing in long-term funds, both debt and equity. These designations leave a category of intermediate-term money represented by debt with from 1 to 5 or 10 years to maturity. Transactions involving such debt are included in our concept of capital-market activity.

row short term by selling commercial paper or by negotiating a bank loan. It may also float a bond issue or sell stock for working capital purposes.

(3) Funds flow back and forth between the two markets, as when the Treasury refinances maturing bills with Treasury bonds or when a bank lends the proceeds of a maturing mortgage to a business firm on short terms.

(4) Some institutions and facilities serve both markets; for example, dealers in short-term Federal securities also buy and sell long-term bonds, and commercial banks make both intermediate- and short-term loans.

(5) Yields in the long- and short-term markets are interrelated. A rise in short-term interest rates reflecting a condition of credit stringency is likely to be accompanied or followed by a rise in long-term rates. Professional investors maintain the normal relationships in the maturity schedule by arbitrage. We should note, however, that money-market rates are more sensitive than longer-term rates and that geographical differences in short-term yields are less pronounced.

Perhaps the chief distinguishing characteristic of the two types of markets is that in the short-term market, as the word "money" suggests, the instruments traded are money or "near money." Federal funds (excess legal reserves of banks) are money. "Near money" instruments are exemplified by short-term government and commercial paper whose value is subject to very slight price risk. The longer-term instruments issued in or traded in the capital markets, especially in the stock market, show considerable price variation.

The Capital Markets: Classification of Characteristics

It is useful to classify the characteristics of the capital markets in several ways.

Major Users: Variety of Types

When funds are made available to those seeking money capital, the latter deliver some kind of contract or instrument representing their relationship with the investors. The demand for funds comes from five general categories of users: individuals, corporations, the Federal government, state and local governments, and foreign borrowers. Individuals rely on the long-term markets for financing real estate and business transactions. All longer-term business debts of individuals and unincorporated concerns, together with the equity in farms and smaller firms, should, in a broad sense of the concept, be included as capital-market contracts. Such components, with the exception of mortgage debt and bank term loans, are omitted from our discussion. This somewhat arbitrary treatment seems valid because measurement is difficult and because such funds are, for the most part, raised locally and in relatively small amounts. Consumer installment debt, e.g., for financing durable goods, is also omitted. This omission is consistent with the exclusion of the durable goods themselves from the economic concept of capital. We are, therefore, left with the mortgage market, both primary and secondary, as the chief type of capital market insofar as individuals are concerned.

Transactions that involve demand for new funds by business corporations, as well as transfers of outstanding corporate instruments, are carried out in two main markets—the corporate note and bond market and the market for corporate stocks. These two are mainly open markets and include both primary and secondary transactions. A market for corporate intermediate-term loans may also be said to exist, but it has no separate identity, being primarily a segment of bank and insurance company loan activity.

As for government securities, our interest lies mainly in the intermediate- and long-term Treasury securities, issued in primary and traded in secondary open markets, and the obligations of state and local jurisdictions, whose market is mainly local and over the counter.

The volume of foreign financing in the American capital markets has become very substantial in the postwar period. The markets for foreign securities are comingled with the domestic corporate bond and stock markets.

Each of these markets has distinctive characteristics of supply and of demand that result in different interest rates and yields. The various segments are, however, interrelated in that they all compete for the supply of funds, and many of the groups seeking funds may choose among the various capital markets to satisfy their financial needs.

Type of Instrument or Contract: Debt or Equity

Most of the instruments that represent funds supplied to and obtained from the capital markets are debt instruments—personal and corporate notes, corporate bonds, and obligations of governments. However, ownership instruments, that is, corporate stocks, are also sold to raise new funds, and outstanding shares are transferred among owners.

Maturity of Instruments

Somewhat arbitrarily, transactions represented by debt instruments with maturity of a year or less are said to take place in the money or short-term market. This leaves intermediate-term funds (up to 5 to 10 years maturity) and long-term funds for the capital markets. As we have seen, the two markets cannot be completely distinguished.

Degree of Centralization

In the broadest sense, the scope of the capital markets is very wide. A market exists wherever a bank or an insurance company makes a term loan, a corporate bond or stock is transferred, a government sells a new bond issue, a householder borrows money on a mortgage. Capital markets are primarily local and regional, except for Federal government securities and the bond and stock markets. Centralization exists insofar as intermediate-term money is concerned, through the concentration of great banking facilities in very large cities. We shall see, however, that geographical barriers are breaking down and that both the supply of and the demand for long-term and even intermediate-term funds tend increasingly to flow on a national basis. Nevertheless, much geographical stratification does persist. Regional and local markets are particularly important for both issuing and trading in obligations of smaller users of funds—local governments, local businesses, and individuals— and in the stocks of smaller corporations.

Direct Versus Open-Market Transactions

When a savings and loan association makes a mortgage loan to a local customer, it is allocating the funds of a number of savers directly to the financing of real estate. The relation between the financial intermediary and the borrower is direct and personal. This is also the case for direct borrowing by governments and corporations and for the private sale of corporate shares by the issuer. Many thousands of direct transactions occur daily between all types of users and suppliers of funds; these transactions are not centrally reported and are competitive only in a very general way. They take place in a vast and segmented market. By contrast, open-market transactions in bonds, stocks, and some mortgages are competitive and immediately influence the open prices of funds, as in the case of a national offering of corporate bonds at a known price and yield or of an issue of Treasury securities.

The line of demarcation between direct (personal) and open-market (impersonal) transactions is not entirely distinct. In general, the latter are characterized by the use of marketing intermediaries—dealers or brokers who bring together the demand and supply of funds, provide transfer facilities, and "make a market" for various instruments. The known yields prevailing in the organized open markets do, however, influence those determined by direct bargaining.

Primary Versus Secondary Transactions

Most transactions in the capital markets represent transfers of existing instruments among investors rather than the raising of new funds. For example, the volume of trading in outstanding securities vastly exceeds the value of new issues. Such mere trading does not represent capital formation. However, the prices and yields at which existing instruments are transferred determine the prices of new issues. Thus, when a corporation offers bonds for new money, their yield must equal or exceed the yield on outstanding bonds of the same quality.

The terms *stock market* and *bond market* usually refer to secondary markets for securities. The term *mortgage market* has, until recently, implied mainly a primary market. Our later discussion includes both the primary and secondary markets for various instruments.

Magnitude of the Markets

Later chapters include discussion of the size of capital markets in terms of the assets and obligations of the institutions involved, the magnitude of various sources and uses of funds, and the flows of funds that influence yields. At this point certain selected data (Table 1-2) are presented to indicate the size of the markets in terms of the outstanding instruments that represent longer-term funds. Individual and noncorporate debt other than mortgage debt is omitted.

United States government debt includes the guaranteed obligations of the Federal Housing Administration. Marketable debt excludes Savings Bonds and other nontransferable instruments. Net long-term debt

Table 1-2. Selected Media in the Capital Market, at Year End, 1950–1968, Billions of Dollars

	1950	1955	1960	1965	1968
United States government debt:					
Total	$257	$281	$290	$321	$358
Marketable	153	163	189	215	237
Federal agency debt (nonguaranteed)	2	4	8	14	22
State and local government debt:*					
Total	24	44	70	100	128‡
Net long-term	21	38	60	86	104‡
Corporate long-term debt:					
Net long-term	60	90	139	209	285
Bonds outstanding	37	58	85	116	157
Corporate stock (market value):					
Listed	111	239	335	573	780‡
Active unlisted‡	†	45	69	130	150‡
Mortgage debt:					
Total	73	130	207	326	397
Residential (1–4 family)	45	88	141	213	251

*June 30.
†Not available.
‡Estimated.
Sources: *Federal Reserve Bulletin* (including flow-of-funds tables); *Treasury Bulletin; Survey of Current Business*; Securities and Exchange Commission, *Annual Reports*; U.S. Department of Commerce, Bureau of the Census, *Governmental Finances* (annual).

of state and local governments excludes sinking funds and intergovern-
mental duplications. Corporate net long-term debt also excludes inter-
company holdings; it includes debt over 1 year to original maturity:
mortgages, term loans, and net long-term trade credit.[9] The figure for
bonds outstanding is most important for our purposes. It excludes
bonds held outside of the United States.

The corporate stock figures are crude in that they include inter-
company ownership of shares. They exclude the value of stock of closely
held companies. Mortgage debt is self-explanatory.

Classification of Institutions

The instruments or contracts that represent claims to or ownership
of assets are issued and traded through a complex of institutions. These
institutions serve as channels through which those needing longer-term
funds draw on the savings of others. Some savings are invested directly
by the savers themselves, and some flow to other users without an intermediary. But for the most part, the savings of millions of saving units
flow to other users through a host of institutions. To quote Kuznets,
"Financial intermediaries obviate the need for each group of savers to
seek out and choose among the wide variety of capital users and, conversely, for each group of capital users to seek out and choose among
the wide variety of savers."[10] We may expand this concept to include
the transfer of already outstanding marketable instruments. The development of institutions has provided a vastly more effective use of savings
and greater liquidity of capital issues.

The American financial system includes a remarkable variety of institutions. In this short book we must confine our attention to those
institutions that form a major part of or serve the various capital markets. These institutions may be classified as follows:

> Deposit institutions:
>> Commercial banks; Federal Reserve banks
>> Mutual savings banks
>> Savings and loan associations
> Insurance and pension institutions:
>> Legal reserve life insurance companies
>> Property and liability insurance companies
>> Noninsured corporate pension funds
>> State and local government retirement funds
>> Federal retirement and insurance funds
> Investment institutions:
>> Investment companies

---

[9] For an explanation of the derivation of net debt, see *Survey of Current Business*
(October 1950), p. 13.

[10] Simon Kuznets, *Capital in the American Economy: Its Formation and Financing*
(Princeton, N.J.: Princeton University Press, 1961), p. 31.

The common characteristic of these institutions is that their assets consist primarily of financial instruments, a substantial portion of which represents intermediate- or long-term debt or equity. The first two groups—deposit and insurance institutions—are further characterized by the fact that their liabilities represent contractual obligations to savers.[11] They are real financial intermediaries, receiving funds from individuals, business, and government, and channeling these funds to users on intermediate or long terms. A net increase in their liabilities (and assets), other than from transfers and market revaluation, reflects a net increase in productive capital and an expansion of economic activity.

Investment companies buy securities of various types and issue bonds or shares against their own portfolios. Although they too hold financial assets, any increase in their portfolios (other than one reflecting a change in market value) represents mainly a transfer to them of debt and equity instruments from other owners.

Certain omissions from the list should be noted. Credit unions are also deposit institutions, but they deal almost exclusively in consumer credit. Fraternal life insurance organizations and the insurance departments of mutual savings banks are relatively small in relation to the "legal reserve" companies, and complete historical data are not available. Bank trustees manage a vast aggregate of assets, but they do not own these assets (in the strict sense) and issue no obligations against them. Investment development companies and small-business investment companies are too specialized to be included in a short book. Sales finance companies obtain some funds in the capital markets, but their activities are confined largely to financing consumer durables.

Federal credit agencies could be classed as a separate institution specializing mainly in mortgage investment. They are discussed in Chapter 7, along with the financing of the Federal government proper.

Two main groups of marketing institutions play a prominent role in the capital markets by serving as middlemen. The first consists of investment bankers and mortgage companies, who merchandise new debt and equity instruments. The second includes securities brokers and dealers, securities exchanges, and mortgage brokers, who aid in the transfer of already outstanding instruments. The work of these marketing types is discussed in Chapters 7 through 11.

---

[11]The exception is the property insurance group whose obligations are not dollar contracts with savers but services owed to customers.

Commercial and Federal Reserve Banks

WE shall first discuss the institutions that accept deposit funds. Their role in the capital markets is to serve as funnels through which savings are invested in intermediate- and long-term instruments. Because of their fiduciary responsibility to depositors, their investment activity is heavily regulated and excludes the acquisition of equities.

Three important deposit institutions are involved in the capital markets: commercial banks, mutual savings banks, and savings and loan associations. Commercial and Federal Reserve banks are discussed in this chapter. Although the Federal Reserve banks are not deposit-type institutions, their relations with commercial banks, their holdings of Federal obligations, and their influence on yields all require our attention.

Commercial Banks

As of January 1969 there were 13,679 commercial banks in the United States, operating approximately 32,500 offices. They fell into three categories: 4,716 national banks, all members of the Federal Reserve System, with total assets of $297 billions; 1,262 state-chartered member banks, with $117 billions in assets; 7,701 state nonmember banks, with $88 billions in assets.

The traditional role of commercial banks was to furnish short-term funds to business, agriculture, and government. However, through the years they have become veritable department stores of finance. Their multifunctional role includes substantial activity in the granting of intermediate-term credit, through term loans, and long-term credit, through the acquisition of government and corporate bonds, and mortgages.

Sources of Funds for Capital-Market Assets

No exact relationship exists between specific sources and uses of bank funds. Funds are derived from demand deposits, savings and time deposits, stockholders' investments, and, recently, from the sale of debentures. But because the turnover of savings and time deposits is so much slower than that of demand deposits (one-half compared with about 30 times per annum), these, together with net worth, constitute the major source for investment in capital-market assets. Time deposits now constitute one-half of total deposits, and their growth has been largely responsible for the shift in bank activity from specialization in short-term financing toward general financing.

Time and savings deposits expanded steadily in the 1950's and 1960's (until 1969), reflecting the general growth of savings in the economy. In the short run, however, these deposits are greatly influenced by the limits placed on the various categories of nondemand deposits by the regulatory authorities (Federal Reserve and Federal Deposit Insurance Corporation). Such limits have at times encouraged, and at other times discouraged, the flow of savings to commercial banks, depending on the rates available at other types of savings institutions and in the open money and capital markets.[1]

Table 2-1 shows the growth of savings and time deposits of all commercial banks from 1950. Data correlated by size and location of banks would show that such deposits are relatively more important for small and medium-sized rural banks than for banks in large cities. At the end of 1968 such deposits amounted to 51 per cent of the total deposits of country bank members of the Federal Reserve System, but only 31 per cent of the total for reserve city banks.

Table 2-1 also includes the growth of capital funds (net worth and debentures) of commercial banks. The appeal of capital-market assets, with their greater price risk, as compared with money-market assets is affected by the relative size of the equity cushion. Other factors include the volatility of demand deposits, the types of loans on the books,

---

[1]Thus, in September 1969, the annual rate on bank pass-book deposits was limited to 4 per cent; single-maturity time deposits (including certificates of deposit) could pay from 5 per cent on less than $100,000 principal to $6\frac{1}{4}$ per cent on $100,000 or more with maturities of 180 or more days. Savings and loan associations were offering 5 per cent on pass-book accounts and $5\frac{1}{4}$ per cent on term accounts. In the open market, U.S. Treasury bills brought 7.1 per cent, and high-grade corporate bonds brought 7.0 per cent.

Table 2-1.   Savings and Time Deposits* and Capital Accounts, All
Commercial Banks, at Year End, 1950–1968, Billions of Dollars

	1950	1955	1960	1965	1968
Savings and time deposits	$36.3	$48.4	$71.6	$146.7	$203.2
Capital accounts	11.6	15.3	21.0	30.3	37.0
Total	$47.9	$63.7	$92.6	$177.0	$240.2

*Excluding interbank deposits.
Source: *Federal Reserve Bulletin.*

the ratio of loans to deposits, the relative yields on short-, intermediate-,
and long-term loans and investments, together with such influences as
the attitude of bank examiners, changes in bank legislation, and the
general need for liquidity of individual banks and of the banking system
as a whole.

Annual Sources of Funds

The annual changes (see Table 2-2) in adjusted savings and time
deposits and capital (at call dates) help to explain the variations in
uses of funds indicated later in this chapter.

The result of the very tight money and capital-market conditions in
1966, which culminated in the "credit crunch" of that fall, was an
unusually small growth of deposits in that year. Rates paid on time and
savings deposits were not competitive with open-market rates or the
interest offered by savings and loan associations. Increases in the allowed
maximum rates of interest helped to reverse the trend in 1967; but, in
1968, commercial banks enjoyed only modest increases in time and
savings deposits, with funds flowing to other uses including open-market
instruments and corporate stock. In 1969 there was a modest but steady
decline in these deposits as competing open-market yields reached
unprecedented heights.

Table 2-2.   Annual Changes in Savings Deposits and Capital, Commercial
Banks, 1960–1968, Billions of Dollars

	1960	1961	1962	1963	1964	1965	1966	1967	1968
Savings and time deposits (adjusted)	$5.0	$12.1	$15.3	$13.4	$15.3	$19.8	$12.1	$23.7	$20.7
Capital accounts	1.4	1.5	1.6	1.6	2.1	2.5	1.8	2.3	2.6
Total	$6.4	$13.6	$16.9	$15.0	$17.4	$22.3	$13.9	$26.0	$23.3

Source: *Federal Reserve Bulletin.*

Commercial banks invest in both money-market and capital-market assets and derive funds from demand deposits as well as from time deposits and capital. Thus, annual changes in the latter two sources cannot properly be called a flow of funds for investment solely in longer-term loans and securities. In some periods, after liquidity requirements have been satisfied, funds from demand deposits are invested in capital-market assets. At the same time, in most years, a substantial portion of time deposits and even net worth is held in liquid form. Shifts among assets also take place, even though their total is not changed.

Because it is not feasible to associate specific sources and uses of bank funds, the actual flow of funds into capital-market instruments must serve as our data on such investments (see p. 24). For 1960–1968, these were as follows (billions of dollars).[2]

1960	1961	1962	1963	1964	1965	1966	1967	1968
$3.7	$10.2	$9.6	$8.1	$9.6	$12.6	$6.1	$22.0	$20.9

By relating these figures to the previous figures of changes in adjusted time deposits and capital accounts, we see that in each year the growth in time deposits and capital accounts was greater than the increase in longer-term assets. The longer-term sources thus provided some funds for cash reserves and short-term assets. The very substantial changes in the annual data, especially the big decline in 1966 and the rebound in 1967–1968, are discussed later in this chapter.

Uses of Bank Funds in the Capital Market: General

When the somewhat arbitrary definition *capital-market financing* (equity investments, intermediate-term debt, and long-term debt) is applied to commercial banking activity, the volume of bank operations in the capital markets is found to be very substantial. They include a variety of direct as well as open-market transactions and involve the whole gamut of users of funds—individuals, business, and government.[3]

---

[2]Derived from data in *Federal Reserve Bulletin*; Federal Deposit Insurance Corporation, *Annual Reports*.

[3]Indirectly, banks will become much more involved in the capital market because of the creation of one-bank holding companies. A rash of conversions of banks to holding companies, the bank becoming the subsidiary, took place in 1968 and 1969. The apparent purpose of this move was to permit the parent to indulge in other activities forbidden to banks per se, including mortgage banking, leasing, operation of mutual funds, and even the travel business. In early 1969, the Administration proposed a bill that would apply the existing Bank Holding Company Act to one-bank systems and subject them to regulation by Federal banking authorities.

Table 2-3, showing the combined assets of all commercial banks since 1950, is a somewhat unrealistic indication of the role of the banks in the capital markets as contrasted with their role in the money market. The data do not distinguish short- and long-term assets. In addition, there is a constant flow of funds between assets with different maturities; the flow is influenced by the need of the banks for liquidity, by the demand for different types of credit, and by the earnings rates on different credit instruments. Transfers from money-market to capital-market assets, and vice versa, are both deliberate and automatic. A bank may sell a long-term Federal bond and invest the proceeds in a short-term bond or make a short-term loan. Or an opposite transaction—from short- to long-term—may be chosen. An automatic shift from long- to short-term takes results from the maturing of loans and investments that, when first acquired, represented intermediate- or long-term credit but that move, with the passage of time, into the short-term maturity schedule.

The asset figures do, however, indicate the important banking functions. The two major categories of "earning assets"—loans and investments—represent, in part, capital-market financing. We shall discuss the

Table 2-3.   Combined Assets of All Commercial Banks, at December Call Dates, 1950–1968, Billions of Dollars

	1950	1955	1960	1965	1968
Cash assets	$ 40.3	$ 46.8	$ 52.2	$ 61.0	$ 84.0
Loans:*					
Commercial and industrial†	21.9	33.2	43.4	71.9	99.0
Farm (excluding real estate)	2.9	4.5	5.7	8.2	9.7
Real estate	13.5	20.8	28.8	49.7	65.7
Individuals (other, including installment)	10.1	17.2	26.5	45.7	58.6
Securities	2.9	5.0	5.1	8.5	10.7
Financial institutions	0.1	0.6	7.7	15.5	16.0
Other	1.4	2.5	2.9	7.3	13.5
Total loans	$ 52.2	$ 82.6	$118.1	$202.8	$268.1
Investments:					
U.S. government securities	62.0	61.6	61.1	59.7	64.7
Bonds of Federal agencies	1.7	1.9	1.8	4.6	10.3
State and local government bonds	8.1	12.7	17.6	38.7	58.7
Corporate bonds	2.2	1.6	0.9	0.9	1.8
Other securities	0.4	0.5	0.6	0.8	1.0
Total investments	$ 74.4	$ 78.3	$ 82.0	$104.7	$136.4
Other assets	2.0	3.0	6.0	10.4	16.1
Total assets	$168.9	$210.7	$258.4	$378.9	$504.6

*Totals show net of reserves.
†Includes commercial paper.
Sources: Federal Deposit Insurance Corporation, *Annual Reports; Federal Reserve Bulletin.*

significance of the intermediate- and long-term portion of each main type of loans and investments, omitting mention of consumer financing even though some of this (e.g., housing improvement loans) may qualify as long term on a strict maturity basis. In general, the earning assets discussed fall outside the "secondary reserves" of the banks—money-market loans and short-term Federal obligations—held primarily for liquidity rather than for income.

Term Loans

The growth in bank term loans has been a most important postwar development. These loans have over 1 year to original maturity (seldom over 10) and are usually amortized on a regular basis. They form part of the commercial loan figure in Table 2-3 and, to a minor extent, the individuals category. Because they lack adequate liquidity, term loans may appear to violate a basic canon of traditional bank loan theory. Their use is justified by their steady amortization and by the general liquidity of the banks. They are alternatives to bond financing by large business concerns and are also used by smaller firms unable to tap the open bond market. They are a desirable replacement for former short-term loans that were continually renewed at maturity. In making term loans, banks compete chiefly with life insurance companies.

Information on the volume and characteristics of bank term loans is irregular and incomplete. The proportion of term to total loans differs greatly among banks; for some large banks it is now over 50 per cent. Very large banks (with deposits of $1 billion or more) held slightly over one-half of the total term loan volume in 1957. But term credits are becoming increasingly important to small business. In 1957 they constituted 46 per cent of all bank loans to borrowers with assets of less than $50,000. This is capital-market financing at the local level. If we assume that the 1957 ratio of term to total loans had prevailed, all commercial banks would have had about $40 billions of such credit outstanding at the end of 1968.[4] This figure may be an understatement. At the end of August 1969, term loans held by large commercial banks (which held 70 per cent of all bank loans) totaled $31 billions, or 40 per cent of their commercial and industrial loans. At this rate the figure for all banks would be over $44 billions.[5]

Term loans to business offer the advantage of flexibility in particular covenants and in type of security required; this flexibility helps to explain their use in financing working-capital and fixed-asset requirements, especially during periods of buoyant business activity and ample

---

[4]The 1957 data were based on the original maturities. As principal is constantly reduced, the amount of outstanding term debt declines unless offset by new loans.

[5]*Federal Reserve Bulletin*, September 1969, p. A31. A new compilation of term loans of large banks has appeared monthly in the *Federal Reserve Bulletin* beginning with the May 1968 issue.

bank credit. But even during periods of credit stringency, the ratio of term to total business loans increases. In such periods, many borrowers, especially smaller firms, turn to these loans when unsecured short-term funds are hard to get. Large firms, waiting for lower long-term rates, finance for shorter periods through term loans. Business firms expect their cash flows (from which term loans are amortized) to be ample regardless of conditions in the financial markets.

Mortgage Financing by Commercial Banks

Table 2-4 shows the composition of bank holdings of mortgages from 1950 through 1968. A substantial concentration in real estate loans is found in banks in the larger metropolitan areas. At the end of 1968,

Table 2-4. Mortgage Loans Held by Commercial Banks,
at Year End, 1950–1968, Billions of Dollars

	1950	1955	1960	1965	1968
Farm	$ 1.0	$ 1.3	$ 1.7	$ 2.9	$ 3.7
Residential:					
1–4-family	9.4	15.1	19.2	30.4	38.8
Multifamily	1.0	0.8	1.1	1.9	2.7
	$10.4	$15.9	$20.3	$32.3	$41.5
Commercial and other	2.3	3.8	6.8	14.5	20.5
Total	$13.7	$21.0	$28.8	$49.7	$65.7
Conventional and other	$ 8.0	$12.7	$20.1	$39.3	$55.1
FHA-insured	3.1	4.6	5.8	7.7	7.9
VA-guaranteed	2.6	3.7	2.9	2.7	2.7
Total	$13.7	$21.0	$28.8	$49.7	$65.7

Sources: *Federal Reserve Bulletin;* Federal Home Loan Bank Board.

total mortgage loans were distributed as shown in Table 2-5 (member banks of the Federal Reserve only).

Table 2-5. Distribution of Bank Mortgage Loans, 1968,
Billions of Dollars

	Amount	Total Mortgage Loans, per cent
182 Reserve city banks in 47 cities	$23.2	46.0
5,796 "Country" banks	27.2	54.0
5,978 Member banks	$50.4	100

Source: *Federal Reserve Bulletin.* Banks in New York and Chicago were central reserve city banks before July 28, 1962; reserve city banks thereafter.

Farm-mortgage loans   Bank loans to farmers are reported in two main categories: real estate loans secured by land and loans exclusive of real estate. The latter category includes some debt that may be classed as capital financing, that is, intermediate-term debt incurred for a variety of purposes, including improvement of land and buildings. The amount of farm loans secured by real estate is regularly reported, and we confine our attention to this item.

Farm mortgages of commercial banks grew from $1 billion in 1950 to $3.7 billions at the end of 1968, when they represented 1.4 per cent of total loans and 0.7 per cent of total assets. The share of the total outstanding farm-mortgage debt held by the banks grew from 10 to 16 per cent in the same period.[6]

As a group, banks are far less important in agricultural real estate financing than are government agencies and life insurance companies. As the size of individual farms increases and as commercial farming becomes more extensive, more capital requirements may be satisfied in the open capital markets, and long-term private farm financing is not confined to direct local negotiations with institutions and individuals.

Home-mortgage loans   In terms of both the number of loans and their dollar amount, bank financing of residential real estate has increased greatly in the postwar years, reflecting the great expansion of activity in housing. Residential 1–4-family mortgage loans held by commercial banks totaled $38.8 billions at the end of 1968 and represented 15 per cent of total bank loans and 8 per cent of total assets, compared with 11 and 2 per cent, respectively, at the end of 1950. At the end of 1968, banks held 15 per cent of the $251 billions of 1–4-family mortgages outstanding in the United States, down from 21 per cent in 1950. Banks have held their relative place, but the biggest increase in dollar volume has gone to savings and loan associations. Of the $38.8 billions of mortgages secured by 1–4-family houses held by banks in 1968, $31 billions, or 80 per cent, consisted of conventional liens. The share of total FHA-insured liens outstanding held by banks declined from 26 per cent in 1950 to 13 per cent in 1968.

The sixfold postwar increase in single-family residential mortgages held by banks reflects the general rise in demand for home financing, the relatively high yields on this type of asset, the great growth in time deposits, and the expansion of Federally underwritten loans. In 1968, national banks were permitted to lend on conventional home mortgages up to 60 per cent of their time deposits or 100 per cent of capital and surplus, whichever was greater. No such restrictions applied to FHA-insured and VA-guaranteed liens. Mortgages as bank invest-

---

[6]Sources: Federal Deposit Insurance Corporation, *Annual Reports*; *Federal Reserve Bulletin*.

ments had fallen into disrepute in the 1930's, but the availability of Federally underwritten liens (with their safety and secondary market), together with the use of amortized payments and longer maturities, led to a substantial shift toward this type of credit. Another factor in this shift has been the increase in the maximum loan-to-value ratio of amortized conventional loans to 75 per cent of appraised value, with a limit of maturity to 20 years. State banking regulations vary from more to less strict than those applying to national banks.

In addition to direct lending on mortgages held to maturity, some banks originate loans that they pass along to others. To a certain degree then, they help to make the mortgage market national in scope. Banks also engage in interim construction financing (the eventual permanent mortgage being acquired by a life insurance company or a mutual savings bank) and in "warehousing," or carrying mortgage loans originated by mortgage companies until the latter pass these along to permanent investors (see Chapter 11).

Multifamily and commercial mortgage loans   Commercial bank holdings of loans on multifamily (apartment) and commercial properties grew from $3.3 billions at the end of 1950 to $23.2 billions in 1968, constituting 9 per cent of total bank loans and 5 per cent of total assets. The 1968 figure represented about 20 per cent of the total of such mortgages outstanding in the United States. The increasing interest in these loans reflects the growth of high-rise housing and the intensive use of commercial land as well as a search by the banks for higher income.

Securities Loans

Although short term, securities loans play an important ancillary role in the securities market. They are made to investment bankers to carry new issues through underwriting and distribution, to dealers for the financing of customers' margin accounts, and to individuals for their purchases of securities.

The volume of securities loans fluctuates with changes in margin requirements, securities prices, the dollar volume of securities trading, the volume of new securities, and interest rates. Margin regulation under the Securities and Exchange Act of 1934, the growth of private placements of securities, and the increased reliance by business on internal financing have all reduced the demand for securities credit. At the end of 1968, outstanding securities loans of all commercial banks totaled $10.7 billions, or 4 per cent of total loans outstanding, compared with the $17 billions outstanding in the autumn of 1929.

Banks also make loans secured by securities collateral—"nonpurpose" loans—for purposes other than purchasing or carrying securities. These are classified as either business or individual loans.

Bank Securities Investments

In the aggregate balance sheets of all commercial banks, loans and investments are classified by major type, not by maturity or purpose. The relative importance of the two main types of earning assets since 1950 is revealed in Table 2-3. At the end of 1950, total investments ($74 billions) were 44 per cent and Federal obligations including bonds of agencies ($62 billions) were 37 per cent of total assets. Total investments reached $136 billions at the end of 1968, but as a result of the great expansion of loans, their proportion of total assets fell to 27 per cent. The $65 billions of Federal securities held at the end of 1968 constituted only 13 per cent of total assets.

Bonds other than United States obligations, with 2 years or less to maturity, constitute the investment portfolio of the banks. These bonds constitute a residual account that provides income from funds not needed for loans and that serves to diversify the assets of the banks. The risk of changing market values is reduced by spacing maturities, although in years like 1968 and 1969, with bond prices at record lows, the potential losses on the sale of bonds contributed greatly to the credit strain and high loan rates. The credit risk (in other than United States obligations) is minimized by applying high investment standards, as required by regulation, and by diversification.

The volume of bond investments is affected by seasonal, cyclical, and secular influences, especially the demand for loans and the available yields on securities compared with interest rates on loans. Federal Reserve policy also affects the ratio of investments to loans. In periods of credit restraint, investments are reduced in order to obtain funds for loan expansion.

United States government securities   Except from the standpoint of income taxation, Treasury obligations are almost ideal bank investments. They involve no credit risk and the least price risk. They can be used as collateral at other banks or at the Federal Reserve banks without penalty rates, have perfect marketability, and are preferred by bank examiners. Shorter maturities provide liquidity as well as safe income, and banks can change the composition of their Federal bond portfolios by shifting between short- and medium-term maturities. In periods of credit ease, banks take the initiative in acquiring medium-term securities for income. Primary reserves are ample and may be expanded by using Federal Reserve credit. In periods of credit strain and higher yields (as in 1959 and 1966 through 1969), securities may be sold to provide loan funds. Such contraction of the investment portfolio is, however, limited by the aversion of the banks to selling the longer maturities at a loss. This critical situation came to a peak in the early summer of 1969 and helped force the prime rate to 8½ per cent.

The longer-run policy of banks is, however, to buy Federal securities in periods of economic recession when the banks have idle funds, even though yields are low and the spread between short- and long-term yields is small (see p. 92). Conversely, they tend, when necessary, to sell bonds in prosperous years at higher yields and lower prices in order to increase loanable funds. This policy almost inevitably leads to losses on resale, which are, however, allowed as expenses for Federal income tax purposes.

Commercial banks are the largest institutional owners of direct and guaranteed United States government securities (see Chapter 7). At the end of 1968, their holdings totaled $65 billions, or 17 per cent of gross Treasury debt, and $53 billions, or 22 per cent, of marketable Federal debt. Bonds with maturities of up to 10 years constituted 91 per cent of marketable Treasury securities held at the end of 1955, 96 per cent at the end of 1960, and 98 per cent at the end of 1963. With a "flat" yield curve beyond 10 years there is little purpose in holding long maturities whose price risk from changing market yields is substantial. When declining interest rates are probable, some new funds may be placed in longer maturities to maximize income. But this situation has not prevailed during the 1960's.

The total dollar amount of bank holdings of Federal securities was fairly stable during the 1950's and most of the 1960's. But in the first nine months of 1969, under great pressure to expand commercial loans, banks reduced their holdings of government obligations by $11.1 billions or 17 per cent. Nevertheless, it is likely that bank investment policy has influenced the spreads between the prices and yields of different maturities of Federal securities rather than the yield structure as a whole.

State and local government obligations   "Municipal" bonds are second only to Federal securities in investment portfolios of banks. In contrast to the decline in Federal bond investments, holdings of state and local government bonds have risen 500 per cent since 1950, and in 1968 totaled $59 billions, or 43 per cent of total investments and 11 per cent of total assets. This increase reflects a number of factors: (1) the great growth of state and local government borrowing since World War II; banks are the principal market for the bonds of smaller municipalities; (2) the attractive yields of "tax exempts" compared to the after-tax yield on other bonds; (3) the good investment record of these bonds; (4) the variety of serial maturities available; (5) the increasing activity of the banks in the underwriting and distribution of municipals.[7] The chief disadvantage of municipals is their lack of a good secondary market. However, most banks hold such securities to maturity. In 1969, when yields on "munis" reached all-time highs and prices reached all-time lows, such a practice was virtually mandatory.

---

[7] Banks are permitted to act as principals in underwriting new municipal issues, excluding revenue bonds.

Banks are not limited in the amount of qualified general tax-supported ("full faith and credit") obligations they are permitted to own. Member banks may own, for portfolio, qualified revenue bonds to the limit of 10 per cent of capital and surplus. In general, the emphasis is on maturities under 10 years; the additional yield on longer maturities is not large enough to offset their greater price risk. Banks adjust their purchases of tax-exempt securities to loan demand and to their reserve position. Changing conditions in these two factors, together with the varying supply of state and local bonds resulting from bond elections, have a pronounced short-run effect on municipal bond yields (see Chapter 8). In the long run, the countercyclical tendency of banks to invest in municipal securities when their own liquidity is high (and interest rates are low) rather than when yields are high provides a supporting influence to this market.

Commercial banks are the largest institutional owners of municipal securities. At the end of 1968, their holdings of $59 billions constituted 46 per cent of total state and local debt (see p. 109).

Corporate bonds   At the end of 1968, commercial banks held $1.8 billions of corporate bonds, constituting only 1.3 per cent of their investments and 0.4 per cent of total assets. This was, however, double the amount held 2 years earlier, reflecting the appeal of the very high interest rates that prevailed in 1967 through 1969. The lack of bank activity in the corporate bond market is explained by the high standards of quality and marketability required by law and regulation for investment in these obligations, by the greater appeal of Federal obligations for safety and liquidity, by the favorable after-tax yields on state and local government bonds, and by the growth of term loans. The demand for corporate bonds by tax-exempt institutions (for example, pension funds) or by those enjoying light income-tax rates (such as life insurance companies) has driven down the yields on high-grade corporate bonds to a level where they are unattractive to the fully taxed banks (see p. 120). Larger issues of high-grade corporate bonds do offer good marketability; but the longer maturities involve more price risk than do alternative investments. Railway equipment obligations, with their serial maturities, are, however, attractive to banks, their principal owners. Despite some recent relaxation of the rules, convertible bonds are not attractive; banks are not allowed to pay more than the "investment" or straight bond value for such securities.

At the end of 1968, commercial banks held only 1.2 per cent of corporate bonds outstanding (see Chapter 9).

Other investments   At the end of 1968, commercial banks held $10.3 billions, or about 30 per cent, of the outstanding bonds (including participation certificates) of United States agencies such as Federal Intermediate Credit Banks, Federal National Mortgage Association, Federal

Land Banks, Banks for Cooperatives, and Federal Home Loan Banks. The yields on these bonds are only slightly higher than those of Treasury obligations because of their moral support by the Federal government and by their good marketability (see p. 99).

Banks are not permitted to buy corporate stocks as investments.[8] They do, however, influence the prices and yields of stocks through the volume of loans used to purchase or to carry securities.

Annual Uses of Funds in the Capital Market, 1960–1968

The annual net changes in bank holdings of capital-market investments are shown in Table 2-6. The data include all maturities of Federal securities. The most pronounced increases are found in multifamily and commercial mortgages and in municipal bonds. As expected, the greatest variation is found in holdings of Treasury securities, which show substantial increases in recession years such as 1961 and substantial decreases in the expansion period of 1962 through 1966.

Table 2-6.   Annual Changes in Capital-Market Assets, Commercial Banks, 1960–1968, Billions of Dollars

	1960	1961	1962	1963	1964	1965	1966	1967	1968
U.S. government bonds	$ 2.1	$ 5.6	$−0.2	$−3.1	$−0.3	$−3.4	$−3.4	$ 6.4	$ 2.2
Federal agency securities	0.4	0.7	0.9	0.5	—	1.1	—	0.5	0.8
State and local government bonds	0.6	2.8	4.4	5.0	3.8	5.1	2.4	9.0	8.1
Term loans to corporations	0.1	−0.3	0.4	0.8	1.3	3.2	2.3	1.5	3.1 (est.)
Corporate bonds	−0.2	−0.2	—	—	0.2	−0.1	0.1	—	—
Home mortgages	—	0.8	2.2	2.8	2.3	3.2	2.4	2.5	3.5
Other mortgages	0.7	0.8	1.9	2.1	2.3	2.5	2.3	2.1	3.2
Total	$ 3.7	$ 10.2	$ 9.6	$ 8.1	$ 9.6	$ 11.6	$ 6.1	$22.0	$20.9

Sources: Federal Deposit Insurance Corporation, *Annual Reports; Federal Reserve Bulletin.* Term loans from Bankers Trust Company, *The Investment Outlook* (New York, annual). Some columns do not add to totals because of rounding.

The variation in savings and time deposits materially influenced the investment policies of the banks. In contrast to such years as 1955 and 1959, banks in 1962 were able to supply rising demands for business, housing, and consumer credit without liquidating Federal securities and were able at the same time to make record increases in their hold-

[8]Exceptions are ownership of stock in Federal Reserve banks by member banks, stock in affiliates, and a few miscellaneous types.

ings of state and local government bonds and mortgages. In 1963 through 1966, however, liquidation of Treasury securities was necessary to increase investment in higher-yielding assets in order to cover the higher interest costs on savings accounts and to accommodate the demand for loans.

The tight money conditions of 1966 are reflected in the data in Table 2-6. Banks reduced their total capital-market use of funds by over 50 per cent. Even the continued liquidation of Federal securities did not relieve the situation. The passing of the "credit crunch" is reflected in the data for 1967, when a substantial investment was made in Federal bonds. As in previous years, holdings of state and local government bonds show the greatest variation. Flow into these investments was sharply reduced in 1966 to provide funds for loans. In 1967, with easing pressure, a record commitment was made in these assets, which were then yielding the highest interest rates in many years (see p. 108). In 1968, capital- and money-market pressure again began to build up, reaching a climax in the summer of 1969. To accommodate the demand for business and mortgage loans, the pace of investment in Federal government bonds was drastically reduced in 1968, and a smaller decline took place in the rate of investment in local government securities. As we have seen, in 1969 the banks sold off rather than bought Federal obligations.

Federal Reserve Banks

Capital-Market Functions

Although the Federal Reserve banks have their greatest direct influence in the short-term money market, some discussion of them is pertinent to our study, on several grounds: (1) these institutions invest some of the funds representing member bank and Treasury deposits in intermediate- and long-term credits and so may be classed as financial intermediaries; (2) the Reserve banks are the third largest institutional owners of United States government obligations; (3) their credit policy has an important impact on the prices and yields of long-term securities and mortgages; (4) their open-market operations in Treasury securities now involve longer-term obligations; and (5) as fiscal agents for the Treasury, they play an important role in the marketing of Federal securities.

Sources of Federal Reserve Funds

Member bank deposits, Treasury deposits, Federal Reserve notes, and capital accounts provide the funds for the investments of the banks in securities and other assets. Member banks are required (1969) to hold 17 or 13 per cent of their demand deposits (depending on their classification as reserve city or country banks) and 3 per cent of their savings and time deposits at the Federal Reserve banks of their districts, less some vault cash counted as reserve.[9] At the end of 1968, member bank reserve deposits totaled $21.8 billions, or nearly 28 per cent of Federal Reserve assets. Their increase since 1945 (from $15.5 billions) reflects the growth of bank deposit liabilities, offset by reductions in member bank reserve requirements. The size of reserve accounts is also influenced by the composition of the deposits of the member banks (demand versus time). Federal Reserve notes outstanding totaled $44.7 billions, or 59 per cent of assets at the end of 1968, while capital stock and other capital accounts totaled $1.3 billions.

Two cautions should be indicated here: (1) It is appropriate to think of the liabilities of the central banks as the result of asset acquisition rather than vice versa. "Federal reserve funds" are supplied by Federal Reserve bank credit outstanding (United States government securities held, discounts and advances, and float), gold stock, and Treasury currency outstanding, and are absorbed by currency in circulation (including Federal Reserve notes), deposits (including reserves of member banks), and minor accounts. (2) In any consolidation of banking system funds, that is, where funds of commercial and central banks are combined, the member bank reserve deposits at the Federal Reserve banks are eliminated to avoid double counting. Such deposits are not additions to the deposits of the member banks on which they are based. For this reason we omit any annual sources of funds data for Federal Reserve banks similar to the data presented for other institutions.

All liabilities of Federal Reserve banks should be considered as very short term, and so their assets must be highly liquid. For this reason, the chief impact of the Reserve banks on the capital markets is more indirect (through other financial intermediaries) than direct.

Uses of Funds: Ownership of United States Government Obligations

The Federal Reserve banks play a direct role in the capital market through their holdings of Federal securities (the only securities they own). Total Federal securities have not increased as much in the 1950's and 1960's as one might suppose—from $20.8 billions, or 44 per cent of total assets in 1950, to $52.9 billions, or 70 per cent at the end of 1968. Annual changes in ownership of direct and guaranteed Federal debt in the period 1960 through 1968 were as follows (billions of dollars):[10]

1960	1961	1962	1963	1964	1965	1966	1967	1968
$0.7	$1.5	$1.9	$2.8	$3.4	$3.8	$3.5	$4.8	$3.8

All Federal securities held are fully marketable, and maturities of 5 years or less constituted 78 per cent of total holdings at the end of 1968.

---

[9]Beginning November 30, 1968, time deposits of over $5 millions required a 6 per cent reserve.

[10]Source: *Federal Reserve Bulletin.*

At that time, the Reserve banks owned $52.9 billions, or nearly 15 per cent of gross and 22 per cent of marketable Federal debt (see Chapter 7). Unlike private lending institutions, Federal Reserve banks do not seek the highest yields. Investment decisions are based on factors other than the availability of profitable outlets for their funds.

Influence on Market Yields

The chief influence of the Reserve banks in the long-term capital markets is through the impact of their credit policy on the loan and investment activities of banks and other financial intermediaries. Changes in the reserve requirements of member banks (sporadic), in the discount rate (more frequent), and in the volume and direction of open-market operations (purchase or sale) of Federal securities (almost continuous) all influence the size of member bank reserve deposits and so encourage the contraction or expansion of member bank lending activity. The second and third of these types of credit control have a specific influence on bank loan rates and other short-term rates in the money market. They influence the volume and yields of intermediate-term loans and mortgages as a part of total bank loans.[11]

The immediate impact of changing Federal Reserve credit policy is felt on short-term interest rates. Thus the increases in the discount rate from $4\frac{1}{2}$ to $5\frac{1}{2}$ per cent in 1968 and to 6 per cent in May 1969 were designed to stiffen short-term market rates as part of the program for curbing credit expansion. The most sensitive short-term rates, those on Treasury bills, serve as bellwether rates for other short-term instruments.

The most continuous tool of credit control is open-market operations. From 1953 to early 1961, the purchases and sales of Treasury obligations directed by the Open Market Committee were concentrated on "bills only." It was felt that any change in short-term interest rates would, through arbitrage and substitution, eventually make itself felt in yields on longer-term Treasury obligations and, by arbitration, on other bond yields. In 1961, the "bills only" policy was abandoned in favor of direct intervention in the long-term markets. But the extent of such intervention has been modest. And the influence of rising short-term rates on longer-term rates is not very significant when the supply of funds seeking long-term investment is large. Thus, in 1962 through 1964, while short-term rates were nudged upward (chiefly through the Treasury policy of emphasizing the sale of short maturities), long-term rates remained much firmer, in line with the desire of the Administration to encourage domestic economic growth. The Federal Reserve banks increased their holdings of long-term Federal bonds substantially in the 1960's to aid in this objective.

---

[11]Changes in the Federal Reserve discount rate have an even more direct effect on the volume of and interest rates on term loans whose contractual rate is tied to the discount rate.

Changes in the general level of interest rates affect the prices of long-term instruments more than those of short-term assets and also lead to shifts among types of assets on the part of investing institutions.[12] A restrictive credit policy that eventually results in higher long-term yields encourages institutions to shift from Treasury issues to the more lucrative mortgages, corporate bonds, and municipal bonds. However, if the flow of savings funds is declining, such shifts are discouraged by the risk of price losses. The volume of forward commitments in mortgages also declines as institutions wait for higher yields in the future.

Marketing Federal Securities

The Reserve banks receive the applications of banks, dealers, and others for new issues of Federal securities, allot them in accordance with Treasury instructions, deliver them, receive payment, and credit the Treasury accounts (see Chapter 7). The banks redeem Federal securities as they mature, pay interest coupons, and otherwise service the debt.

---

[12]A change from a 5 per cent to a 6 per cent yield would cause the price of a 1-year obligation selling at par to drop to 99.04; a 20-year 5 per cent bond selling at par would decline to 88.44.

Savings Banks and Associations

THIS chapter discusses the two types of savings institutions that emphasize investment in mortgages. Since mutual savings banks and savings and loan associations do not accept demand deposits and since the turnover of their savings accounts is relatively slow, they invest primarily in capital-market instruments. The chief financial difference between the two is that the savings banks have greater liquidity through more emphasis on Federal and high-grade corporate bonds.

Mutual Savings Banks

General Nature and Functions

At the beginning of 1969, there were 500 mutual savings banks chartered in 18 states (mostly in the middle Atlantic states and New England and one in the Virgin Islands) with total assets of $71.1 billions. Nearly three-quarters of the banks were located in 3 states (New York, Massachusetts, and Connecticut) and held over four-fifths of the combined assets. There were 11 banks in the Midwest and 10 in the Pacific Northwest and Alaska. Including 848 branches, 1,350 offices were operated, serving 23.3 million deposit accounts.

Mutual savings banks are the only deposit institution functioning solely under state charter. They are owned by depositors, who receive

29

all earnings after provision for adequate reserves. Management is in the hands of boards of trustees.

Two basic functions of a mutual savings bank are to serve as a safe depository for the thrift savings of individuals and to invest funds for the maximum yield consistent with safety. Ancillary activities include the sale of life insurance by banks in New York, Massachusetts, and Connecticut.

Sources of Investment Funds

Time deposits provide the funds for over 90 per cent of assets. The balance, general reserve accounts, consists of retained earnings reserved by law (such as the "Surplus Fund" in New York banks) or restricted by management, plus contingency reserves and undivided profits.[1] The ratio of general reserve accounts to deposits is the basic measure of safety. For all banks it averaged 8.1 per cent at the end of 1968. The ratio falls during periods of rapid deposit expansion. Annual additions to these reserve accounts have averaged 8.6 per cent of net operating income in the 1960's. (See Table 3-1.)

From 1950 through 1968, the total deposits of mutual savings banks increased from $20 billions to $65 billions, or 225 per cent. Their turnover is relatively slow at one-third times a year, or about half that of savings accounts of commercial banks.[2] Changes in the amount of deposits in mutual savings banks are functions of the rates of individuals' savings, of their preferences for various media of savings, and of interest rates paid. During the postwar period, growth of deposits has fallen somewhat behind the growth of savings accounts of commercial banks and reserves of life insurance companies, and sharply behind the growth of accounts in savings and loan associations. This falling behind stems from their lack of national exposure, from the specialized functions they perform, and from the lower interest rates paid on deposits.

Table 3-1.   Combined Deposits and Reserve Accounts of Mutual Savings Banks, at Year End, 1950–1968, Billions of Dollars

	1950	1955	1960	1965	1968
Deposits (time)	$20.0	$28.2	$36.4	$52.4	$64.5
General reserves	2.2	2.8	3.6	4.7	5.3
Total	$22.2	$31.0	$40.0	$57.1	$69.8

Sources: *Federal Reserve Bulletin*; National Association of Mutual Savings Banks, *Mutual Savings Banking, National Fact Book* (New York, annual).

[1] In our balance sheet data, reserves against securities and mortgages are deducted from the value of assets to which they belong.

[2] National Association of Mutual Savings Banks, *Mutual Savings Banking, National Fact Book* (New York, 1969), p. 15.

Annual Sources of Funds

The annual increases in deposits and net worth accounts from 1960 through 1968 were as shown in Table 3-2.

The increases in deposits have not been uniform, showing something of a cyclical pattern (as in 1965–1966). Nevertheless, these banks have annually provided substantial funds to the capital markets. The increases in 1962 through 1964 reflect the raise made in interest rates paid on time deposits to compete with those paid on bank savings accounts. The drastic decline in 1966, although reflecting sluggish business conditions, was chiefly attributable to the turbulence in the money and capital markets that culminated in the "credit crunch" in October. General funds dried up, and commercial banks (on certificates of deposit) and direct open-market investment instruments siphoned off individuals' savings from thrift institutions. Interest rates rose to the highest levels in 40 years. To meet severe strains on liquidity and earnings in 1966, mutual savings banks were able to draw on the significant reserves built up in previous years to maintain internal strength.

In 1967, individuals shifted substantial funds from open-market instruments into savings accounts. Monetary policy was one of ease until the autumn, when the rise in the Federal Reserve discount rate and record yields on open-market obligations caused the rate of savings to decline. Even so, for the year as a whole, the deposits of mutual savings banks increased over $5 billions.

Money and capital-market strain was felt again in 1968, when the general interest rates rose sharply. The flow of funds into mutual savings banks was strong, but down somewhat from that of 1967. In 1969, as open-market short- and long-term yields reached historical highs, the flow of savings into mutual savings bank deposit accounts decelerated substantially. In contrast to the $4 to $5 billions annual increase in previous "normal" years, deposits grew only $2.0 billions in the first 9 months. "Disintermediation," or the flow of savings to the open markets, reflected the greater appeal of high-yielding bonds and of equities, especially mutual funds.

Table 3-2.   Annual Changes in Deposits and Reserves, Mutual Savings Banks, 1960–1968, Billions of Dollars

	1960	1961	1962	1963	1964	1965	1966	1967	1968
Deposits	$1.4	$1.9	$3.1	$3.3	$4.2	$3.6	$2.6	$5.1	$4.4
General reserves	0.2	0.2	0.2	0.2	0.2	0.3	0.2	0.1	0.3
Total	$1.6	$2.1	$3.3	$3.5	$4.4	$3.9	$2.8	$5.2	$4.7

Sources: National Association of Mutual Savings Banks, *Mutual Savings Banking, National Fact Book* (annual); *Federal Reserve Bulletin.*

Reserves have failed to keep pace with the growth of deposits because of the increase in interest rates paid on savings and because Federal income taxes now apply to a portion of the credits to reserves. Deducting from the figures in Table 3-2 the net changes in cash and miscellaneous assets produces the following annual sources of new funds available for investment in capital-market assets:

1960	1961	1962	1963	1964	1965	1966	1967	1968
$1.5	$2.0	$3.3	$3.5	$4.2	$3.7	$2.5	$5.3	$4.6

Such data on net changes do not represent the amount of funds actually used in capital-market transactions. The amortization of mortgages and the maturing of bonds, together with investment income, produce substantial additional funds for reinvestment.

General Investment Policy

The basic purposes of savings banks require that conservative policies of lending and investment be followed. Maximizing earnings is of secondary importance. Although deposits turn slowly, a substantial degree of liquidity must be maintained. The importance of the ultimate safety of assets explains the strict legal requirements that govern investment in securities and mortgages in the various states.[3] These specify the eligible instruments, the standards of quality applied to each (except Federal obligations, which automatically qualify), and the limitations on some major instruments as percentages of total assets or total deposits. In two states (Maryland and Delaware), the prudent-man rule applies; this rule, in theory, permits broad discretion but in fact results in the acquisition of high-grade investments. Legal restrictions limit the demand for certain securities (such as industrial bonds) and for mortgages, especially those originating out of state. This limitation restricts the flow of funds through the national capital markets and contributes to the differential yields among different categories of investments.

Table 3-3 shows the amounts and distribution of industry assets for selected years beginning in 1950. During this period, major shifts took place in the investment powers of savings banks and in their role in the capital markets. Their most important impact is seen in the reversal of the position of Federal securities and mortgages, even during a substantial increase in total assets.

The data in Table 3-3 do not reveal the interim cyclical changes in

---

[3]For a convenient discussion of legal lists, see National Association of Mutual Savings Banks, *Mutual Savings Banking: Basic Characteristics and Role in the National Economy*, a monograph prepared for the Commission on Money and Credit (Englewood Cliffs, N.J.: Prentice-Hall, Inc., 1962), Chap. 5.

Table 3-3. Combined Assets of Mutual Savings Banks, Amounts and Percentages, at Year End, 1950–1968, Billions of Dollars

	1950		1955		1960		1965		1968	
Cash assets	$ 0.8	3.6%	$ 1.0	3.2%	$ 0.9	2.2%	$ 1.0	1.5%	$ 1.0	1.4%
Real estate loans (net)	8.0	35.7	17.4	55.6	26.9	66.2	44.4	76.2	53.3	75.0
U.S. government bonds	10.8	48.2	8.5	27.2	6.2	15.3	5.5	9.4	3.8	5.3
Federal agency securities	—	—	0.1	0.3	0.5	1.2	0.8	1.4	1.6	2.2
State and local government bonds	0.1	0.4	0.6	1.9	0.7	1.7	0.3	0.5	0.2	0.3
Corporate and other bonds	2.2	9.8	2.6	8.3	3.8	9.4	2.9	5.3	6.6	9.3
Preferred stocks	—	—	—	—	0.3	0.8	0.4	0.7	0.6	0.9
Common stocks	0.2	1.0	0.6	1.9	0.5	1.2	1.0	1.8	1.4	2.0
Other assets	0.3	1.3	0.5	1.6	0.8	2.0	1.8	3.2	2.6	3.6
Total	$22.4	100	$31.3	100	$40.6	100	$58.2	100	$71.1	100

Sources: *Federal Reserve Bulletin;* National Association of Mutual Savings Banks, *Mutual Savings Banking, National Fact Book* (annual).

flow of funds into assets that reflected variations in relative yield differentials among alternative capital-market instruments, especially the differences between the changing yields on corporate and municipal bonds and the relatively inflexible yields on Federally underwritten mortgages. During periods of credit stringency, such as 1956 through 1957 and 1966 through 1969, the emphasis on new investment was in the former category as the spread in yields declined; during periods of credit ease and of lower yields, the emphasis was on mortgages (see pp. 143–44).

The relative importance of major types of assets varies considerably among banks domiciled in different states because of differences in legal list requirements, strictness of supervision, need for liquidity, rate of supply of funds, and local investment opportunities. For example, the banks in New York State have the highest percentage of assets in mortgages (78 per cent in 1968) and those in Pennsylvania the highest percentage in corporate securities (22 per cent); those in Massachusetts have the highest percentage in United States government securities (10 per cent in 1968).[4] A major purpose of the drive for Federal chartering of mutual banks that culminated in a specific bill (not yet passed) was to broaden and unify investment powers and to make funds available in a wider national market.

[4]National Association of Mutual Savings Banks, *Mutual Savings Banking, National Fact Book* (1969), p. 3.

Securities Investments

Savings banks have played a relatively minor role in the securities markets in recent years. Total securities were $13.3 billions, or 60 per cent of total assets, in 1950; and $14 billions, but only 20 per cent, in 1968. The shift was away from low-yielding Treasury securities and toward a great new emphasis on mortgages. The absence of commercial bank reserve requirements and the lesser need for liquidity meant that less emphasis need be placed on cash and that secondary reserves could consist of longer-maturity Federal bonds. Unlike life insurance companies, which acquire corporate bonds by private placements, savings banks obtain these securities mainly in the open market and so are able to turn to that market for funds when resale is indicated. The pressure for ultimate safety requires such standards for corporate bonds that Federal obligations dominate the securities portfolio. However, shifting between bonds and mortgages and among bonds does occur, reflecting changes in available funds and in the relative yields on different investments.

United States government securities   Federal obligations are held for safety, liquidity, and income. They reached their peak at the end of World War II because of the efforts of the banks to aid in war financing and the lack of a good supply of mortgages and corporate bonds. The great postwar movement into the higher-yielding mortgages reduced the combined holdings of Federal obligations from $10.7 billions, or 63 per cent of total assets, in 1945 to $3.8 billions, or only 5 per cent of total assets, at the end of 1968.

Savings banks have traditionally held Federal securities for liquidity rather than for earnings. Bonds with a maturity of 5 years or less have increased from $0.9 billion in 1945, or 8.4 per cent of marketable Federal securities held, to $1.8 billions, or 51 per cent of such bonds, in 1968. This shift reflects the more favorable yields available on the shorter maturities in recent years as well as the need to avoid price risk and thus help offset the growing emphasis on mortgages.

Other securities investments   Holdings of bonds of Federal credit agencies have shown a modest increase in recent years and stood at $1.6 billions at the end of 1968. Holdings of corporate and foreign bonds have increased both relatively and absolutely in the postwar period. At the end of 1968, they totaled $6.6 billions, or 9.3 per cent of total assets. Investment in such securities varies with the demand for and yields on mortgages, especially on FHA-insured and VA-guaranteed liens, compared with bond yields. In years like 1963 and 1964, corporate bond investments decreased; they increased in 1960 and from 1967 through 1969; in the latter years, bond yields were increasingly attractive, although in 1968 the pressure for mortgage loans cut back the rate of bond acquisition. At the end of 1968, mutual savings banks held 4.2 per cent of total corporate bonds outstanding.

The acquisition of state and local government bonds increased after 1951, when the banks were made subject to Federal income taxation (on earnings over allowed bad-debt reserves). These investments declined in the 1960's, as other yields proved more attractive, and constituted less than 0.3 per cent of total assets at the end of 1968. The purchase of corporate stocks was given impetus in 1951 by the imposition of income taxation, giving dividend income (which is 85 per cent exempt) a special appeal, and by changes in state law such as when New York in 1952 made modest amounts of selected common stocks eligible for purchase. At the end of 1968, savings banks held $2.0 billions of corporate stocks (at year-end market value), comprising $0.6 billion preferred and $1.4 billions common.

Mortgages: general policy   Sound mortgages are almost ideal investments for mutual savings banks. Needed liquidity is provided by holdings of Federal securities and by careful management of cash flows. At the end of 1968, mutual savings banks held $53.4 billions, or 13 per cent, of the total outstanding mortgage debt of $398 billions and $35 billions, or 14 per cent, of the $251 billions of the 1–4-family residential debt outstanding. Real estate loans constituted 75 per cent of their combined assets. Within the industry, the percentage of mortgage assets varied among different banks from less than one-half to over 80 per cent.

In 1968, the emphasis on mortgages as assets was the highest in the history of mutual savings banks. The big postwar growth in mortgages (see Table 3-4) reflects a number of factors: (1) the increase in deposits

Table 3-4.   Mortgage Loans Held by Mutual Savings Banks, at Year End, 1950–1968, Billions of Dollars

	1950	1955	1960	1965	1968
Farm	*	*	*	*	$ 0.1
Residential:					
1–4-family	$4.3	$11.1	$18.4	$30.2	$35.0
Multifamily	2.7	4.5	5.9	10.1	11.7
	$7.0	$15.6	$24.3	$40.3	$46.7
Commercial and other	1.2	1.8	2.6	4.3	6.6
Total	$8.3	$17.4	$26.9	$44.6	$53.4
Conventional and other	$5.2	$ 7.5	$10.9	$19.4	$25.8
FHA-insured	1.6	4.1	7.0	13.8	15.6
VA-guaranteed	1.5	5.8	9.0	11.4	12.0
Total	$8.3	$17.4	$26.9	$44.6	$53.4

*Less than $100 millions.
Sources: *Federal Reserve Bulletin;* National Association of Mutual Savings Banks, *Mutual Savings Banking, National Fact Book* (annual).

and therefore of assets in general; (2) the great postwar demand for housing credit; (3) the development of amortized Federally under-written liens; (4) the relatively attractive yields on mortgages as com-pared with securities; (5) the liberalization of regulations governing investment in mortgages; loan-to-value ratios for conventional mort-gages have risen to 70–75 per cent in most states of domicile; (6) the increasing practice of out-of-state lending that began in 1949–1950, which has been facilitated by greater use of local mortgage company correspondents.

The typical mutual savings bank seeks to maximize its earnings (and hence the rate paid to depositors) by setting as high a ratio of mortgages to total assets as regulation and local demand require and by seeking outside outlets for mortgages funds, depending on available funds and on whether policy requires emphasis on local financing. Funds are allocated to mortgage investment a year or so in advance on the basis of the expected inflow of deposits and repayments of principal, and forward commitments are made with the correspondents who originate a large portion of the liens (see Chapter 11). The secondary market is frequently used to fulfill immediate portfolio requirements.

Emphasis on residential mortgages   Investment in farm and com-mercial mortgages is negligible. At the end of 1968, holdings of farm, commercial, and miscellaneous liens totaled $6.7 billions, but these constituted only 12 per cent of all mortgage investments. However, their relative importance is growing (see p. 38).

Residential loans have grown from $7.6 billions, or 85 per cent of total mortgages held, at the end of 1950 to $46.7 billions, or 88 per cent, at the end of 1968. The biggest rise is found in 1–4-family liens, which, at the end of 1968 totaled $35.0 billions and constituted two-thirds of total loans. Although multifamily residential liens have risen steadily in dollar amount (to $11.7 billions at the end of 1968), they have declined to about one-fifth of total mortgage loans.

Mutual savings banks are the largest single source of Federally under-written home loans. At the end of 1968, they held $27.6 billions of FHA-insured and VA-guaranteed mortgages, or nearly one-third of the combined total. These mortgages rose in percentage of total mortgages held from one-tenth in 1945 to over 50 per cent by 1968. Substantial purchases of mortgages originating in capital-deficient areas have swelled the total.

Although there is some turnover in their mortgage portfolio, savings banks usually hold their original loans to maturity. Turnover is affected by the relative yields available on corporate and Federal securities and by the relation between yields on conventional liens, which reflect market conditions, and those on Federally underwritten loans, which are more static.

The lag of nominal (contractual) yields on FHA-insured mortgages behind open-market yields has slowed down the growth of investment in such instruments, and outstanding VA-guaranteed liens have steadily declined as amortization has outstripped new holdings. The increase in the contractual rate to its peak of 8½ per cent in December 1969 was designed to maintain interest in Federally sponsored liens, but continued increases in market yields left these liens in a poor competitive position (see p. 139).

Annual Uses of Funds in the Capital Market

The data in Table 3-5 show the annual changes in capital-market investments for 1960 through 1968. The home-mortgage figure is volatile, reflecting net changes in deposits and in the varying attractiveness of other assets in various years. The decrease in multifamily and commercial mortgages since 1964 is noteworthy, as is the steady sell-off of Federal obligations.

The credit squeeze in 1966 is readily apparent. Liquidation of Federal bonds was not sufficient to permit a continued increase in mortgages. In 1967, the latter rose modestly, but the big swing was to corporate bonds, to take advantage of their high yields and superior marketability. In 1968 and 1969, the rate of acquisition of home mortgages

Table 3-5. Annual Changes in Capital-Market Assets of Mutual Savings Banks, 1960–1968, Billions of Dollars

	1960	1961	1962	1963	1964	1965	1966	1967	1968
U.S. Government securities	$—0.6	$—0.1	—	$—0.2	$—0.1	$—0.3	$—0.7	$—0.4	$—0.5
Federal agency securities	0.1	—	0.1	0.1	0.1	—	0.2	0.2	0.4
State and local goverment bonds	—	—	—0.2	—0.1	—	—0.1	—0.1	—	—
Foreign securities	—	—	—	—0.1	—	—	—	0.2	0.1 (est.)
Corporate bonds	0.1	—0.1	—	—0.2	—0.2	—0.1	0.3	1.9	1.3
Corporate stocks	—	0.1	0.2	0.1	0.1	0.1	0.1	0.2	0.2
Home mortgages	1.5	1.7	2.1	2.7	2.7	2.8	1.5	1.9	1.6
Other mortgages	0.5	0.5	1.1	1.2	1.6	1.3	1.2	1.3	1.4
Total	$1.5	$2.0	$3.3	$3.5	$4.2	$3.7	$2.5	$5.3	$4.6

Sources: National Association of Mutual Savings Banks, *Mutual Savings Banking, National Fact Book* (annual); Bankers Trust Company, *The Investment Outlook* (New York, annual). Some columns do not add to totals because of rounding.

slowed down, reflecting not only a lower total supply of funds but also the more attractive yields on multifamily and commercial mortgages. And in contrast to the previous annual increase of $3 to $4 billions in mortgages held, in the first 9 months of 1969 these assets rose only $1.9 billions.

Savings Banks in the National Capital Markets

Savings banks play a relatively minor role in the Federal securities market, and their impact on the corporate bond market is even smaller. They have their greatest influence in the mortgage market. Interstate lending, formerly dominated by life insurance companies, has achieved major proportions. At the end of 1968, mortgages secured by property located in states other than states of domicile reached $15 billions, or 29 per cent of total mortgages held. Most out-of-state loans are acquired from mortgage companies that retain the servicing of the loans (see Chapter 11). Relaxed regulations permitting out-of-state loans, together with the growing use of correspondents, have done much to break down geographical barriers. Many smaller banks confine their lending operations to their local communities. But the larger eastern banks are active exporters of capital to capital-deficient areas such as the Southwest and the West.

Savings and Loan Associations

Savings and loan associations are the only major financial institutions expressly designed to make home-mortgage loans. At the end of 1968, they held $131 billions in mortgages. Their assets grew from $8.7 billions in 1945 to $152.8 billions at the end of 1968—an average of over $6 billions per year. Associations operate almost exclusively in the long-term markets, with activity confined mostly to the financing of local housing.

Savings and loan associations are organized under both Federal and state charters. The savings accounts of all Federally chartered associations are insured (to $20,000 per account) by the Federal Savings and Loan Insurance Corporation. State-chartered associations may join the Corporation. Federal and insured state associations are regulated by the Federal Home Loan Bank Board, and uninsured state associations, by the Federal Home Loan Bank Board and state regulatory departments. At the end of 1968, there were 2,063 Federally chartered associations with assets of $81.1 billions, and 3,933 state-chartered associations with assets of $71.7 billions.

All Federally chartered associations are mutual, without stockholders. Capital stock associations are permitted in 21 states, in three of which— California, Ohio, and Texas—they control over 80 per cent of stock association assets. In these states, holding companies control approximately 65 associations (1961).[5]

In January 1969, the Federal Home Loan Bank Board issued regulations permitting Federally chartered associations (and state-chartered mutual associations where state laws permit) to be classified as "deposit institutions." Holders of "savings accounts" were to be considered creditors in every sense of the term. (Depositors would, however, retain their voting privileges.) One result of the ruling was that such associations can offer, in addition to pass-book accounts, a variety of savings arrangements, including fixed-rate deposit certificates up to 5 years in maturity.

Major Function

Savings and loan associations are the most important single source of home-mortgage credit. Their great growth in the postwar period and their emphasis on mortgage financing are revealed in Table 3-7 (p. 41). Real estate loans (including property-improvement loans) constitute 85 per cent of their combined assets. The bulk of the mortgages are conventional liens secured by 1–4-family dwellings.

General Sources of Funds

Unlike commercial and mutual savings banks, savings and loan associations have a direct relationship between the major sources and uses of funds. One source—savings—and one use—real estate financing—predominate and are of approximately equal importance. The savings accounts of these associations increased from $14 billions in 1950 to $132 billions at the end of 1968, when they constituted 86 per cent of total liabilities. The other liabilities were advances from Federal Home Loan Banks, $5.3 billions; general reserves, undivided profits, and capital stock and surplus (stock associations), $10.3 billions; and miscellaneous liabilities, including loans in process, $2.9 billions.

At the end of 1968, savings accounts represented 32 per cent of balances in all deposit institutions—an increase from $14 billions, or 19 per cent, in 1950. The absolute and relative growth is attributable to (1) the general national increase in deposit savings of all types; (2) the higher rates paid to savers (generally 0.5 to 1 per cent above rates on bank savings deposits in the same localities)[6]; and (3) aggressive promotion. Savings and loan savings accounts are akin to bank time de-

---

[5]L. T. Kendall, *The Savings and Loan Business*, a monograph prepared for the Commission on Money and Credit (Englewood Cliffs, N.J.: Prentice-Hall, Inc., 1962), p. 11.

[6]From 1965 through 1969, commercial bank certificates of deposit paid equal or higher rates of interest and increased at a faster rate than did savings capital in savings and loan associations.

posits, but their turnover is much slower. In 1968, savings funds turned over once every 3 years and 2 months.[7] This justifies the concentration of investment in long-term and nonliquid assets.

The protection to savings and loan account holders afforded by reserves and capital (7.7 per cent of savings accounts in 1968) is about the same as that provided by commercial banks (see Chapter 2).[8] However, safety is better measured by the quality and liquidity of assets than by their dollar relationship to liabilities.

Annual Sources of Funds

Annual sources of net funds for 1960 through 1968, derived by changes in balance sheet items, are shown in Table 3-6. There was an increase in annual sources, accelerated in 1962 and 1963 by increased rates paid on savings capital to compete with new higher rates on commercial bank savings and time deposits, until 1964. The pace of savings accumulation declined modestly in 1964 and 1965 and shrank to an all-time low (for the 1950's and 1960's) in the crisis year of 1966 because of the greater appeal of bank certificates of deposit and open-market securities. In 1967, the growth of savings capital resumed its former pace. A lag in the revival of mortgage lending increased

Table 3-6.   Sources of Net Funds, Savings and Loan Associations, 1960–1968, Billions of Dollars

	1960	1961	1962	1963	1964	1965	1966	1967	1968
Savings accounts	$7.6	$ 8.7	$ 9.4	$11.1	$10.5	$ 8.4	$3.6	$10.5	$7.1
Reserves, undivided profits, and capital	0.6	0.7	0.8	0.7	0.7	0.8	0.4	0.5	0.7
Borrowing	—0.1	0.7	0.8	1.4	0.6	0.8	1.0	—2.7	1.0
Loans in process	—0.1	0.4	0.4	0.5	—0.3	—	—1.0	1.0	0.2
Total	$7.9	$10.5	$11.4	$13.7	$11.6	$10.0	$4.0	$ 9.3	$9.0

Sources: United States Savings and Loan League, *Savings and Loan Fact Book* (annual); *Federal Reserve Bulletin;* Bankers Trust Company, *The Investment Outlook* (New York, annual). Some columns do not add to totals because of rounding.

[7]United States Savings and Loan League, *Savings and Loan Fact Book, 1969,* (Chicago: The League, 1970), p. 71.

[8]Beginning in 1966, the Federal House Loan Bank Board required that associations with adjusted net worth (actual net worth less an allowance for delinquent mortgages) between 8 and 10 per cent of specified assets (conventional loans plus 20 per cent of FHA and VA loans) allocate 5 per cent of net income to reserves each year. Those with adjusted net worth of less than 8 per cent of specified assets were required to allocate the higher of this amount or 6 per cent of the growth in loans. The latter part of this formula was suspended for one year in May 1969 to encourage greater mortgage lending.

liquid funds. Borrowing from the Federal Home Loan Banks, which had been substantial in 1966, was nonexistent in 1967, when large net payments were made on such debt. The accumulation of net worth was reduced in 1966 and 1967 because of lower earnings and higher rates of Federal income taxes. In 1968, the flow of net savings into the associations fell off as a result of "disintermediation"—funds found their way into open-market securities with higher yields. Net savings receipts continued to decline in 1969. In the first nine months of that year they totalled only $3.0 billions.

Deducting annual changes in cash and miscellaneous assets from the figures in Table 3-6 provides data on the funds available for capital market investment:

1960	1961	1962	1963	1964	1965	1966	1967	1968
$7.1	$9.4	$10.3	$13.1	$11.1	$9.6	$4.6	$9.3	$9.6

Uses of Funds: General Investment Policy

That savings and loan associations are primarily mortgage-lending agencies is revealed by Table 3-7, which shows the composition of industry assets from 1950 through 1968. They attract savings for this purpose. They do not make commercial loans (except construction loans) and do not accept demand deposits. They need and have much less liquidity than do commercial banks. The return offered to savers (4 to 5¼ per cent in 1968) is competitive with or exceeds the yields on bank deposits and contributes to a slow turnover of accounts. At the end

Table 3-7.   Combined Assets of Savings and Loan Associations, Amounts and Percentages, at Year End, 1950–1968, Billions of Dollars

	1950	Per Cent	1955	Per Cent	1960	Per Cent	1965	Per Cent	1968	Per Cent
U.S. government bonds	$ 1.4	8.8	$ 2.3	6.1	$ 4.6	6.4	$ 7.4	5.7	$ 9.5	6.2
Federal agency securities	0.1	—	0.1	—	0.4	0.6	0.7	0.5	1.4	0.9
Mortgage loans	13.7	81.1	31.5	83.8	60.1	84.1	110.3	85.1	130.8	85.6
Federal Home Loan Bank stock	0.2	1.2	0.5	1.3	1.0	1.4	1.3	1.0	1.4	0.9
Cash	1.0	5.4	2.1	5.6	2.7	3.8	3.9	3.0	2.9	1.9
Other assets	0.5	3.5	1.1	3.2	2.7	3.7	6.0	4.6	6.8	4.5
Total	$16.9	100	$37.6	100	$71.5	100	$129.5	100	$152.8	100

Sources: Federal Home Loan Bank Board; United States Savings and Loan League, *Savings and Loan Fact Book* (annual).

of 1968, for all associations combined, cash and United States government securities showed a ratio of 9.5 per cent to savings accounts;[9] the decline in percentage since 1950 reflects the great growth in housing activity, the demand for mortgage financing in the postwar period, and the increasing role of associations in this area.

Such low liquidity would be a matter of more concern if it were not for the availability of funds from the regional Federal Home Loan Banks. At the end of 1968, all Federally chartered associations and 2,786 associations with state charters, together representing 98 per cent of the assets of the industry, were members of the Federal Home Loan Banking system and had obligations to the banks of $5.3 billions, or 4 per cent of savings balances. Loans from the Federal Home Loan Banks are used to smooth irregularities among savings inflow, withdrawals, and mortgage-lending activity. Reliance on the bank of their district varies greatly among associations. In addition to lending to member associations at varying rates of interest, the Banks serve as general regulatory agencies. Their policies with respect to the amount of credit extended and the rates on same, as well as their dictates on maximum interest to be paid on member savings accounts, have a very substantial influence on member lending policies.

Liquidity requirements are also determined by the seasonal pattern of deposits and withdrawals and by the flow of cash derived from maturing mortgages. These factors differ considerably among associations.

Safety, or ultimate debt-paying ability, is an important factor for all financial institutions. It is a function of liquidity, quality of earning assets, and the relation of net worth to liabilities. For savings and loan associations, concentration on home mortgages means that both earning power and debt-paying ability depend on the development and management of these assets (to a large degree, so does the growth, stability, and yield pattern in the whole home-mortgage market, in which the associations are the most important element). The associations play a leading role in equating the supply of savings available and the demand for mortgage loans. During years such as 1966 and 1968, when the inflow of savings declined or slowed down, investment in Federal securities was reduced, and Federal Home Loan Bank advances were used heavily. In other years, such as 1967, when loan demand slowed down, liquid assets were increased. From 1950 through 1968, mortgages on 1–4-family houses never fell below 70 per cent or rose above 80 per cent of total assets, although the latter were constantly increasing in dollar amount.

Savings and loan associations may lend only the savings they attract (plus a modest amount of borrowed funds). But like banks, they must

---

[9]Members of the Federal Home Loan Bank system (Federally chartered associations and most large state-chartered associations) are required (June 1969) to maintain cash and Government securities of at least 6 per cent of total savings balances.

offer appealing rates to attract savings—higher yields than their competition does. A fully invested position in mortgages is required for such yields to be earned and modest profits made.

Because they concentrate on mortgage lending in their own localities, associations have no great need for a flexible investment policy that reflects changes in general capital-market conditions. They shift among different media and markets to a minor degree only.

Mortgage Lending

The great postwar rise in total mortgage investments has been spectacular, reflecting both the national increase in total home mortgages and the increase in the share of deposit savings and home financing held by associations. Table 3-8 shows that the bulk of mortgage loans are (amortized) conventional loans on 1–4-family housing units. Changes in relative amounts since 1950 are seen in an increase in the proportion of multifamily to total residential loans and in an increase in Federally underwritten loans. But at the end of 1968, loans on 1–4-family homes still constituted 84 per cent of total mortgages (and 70 per cent of total assets).

Savings and loan associations specialize in amortized conventional residential loans for the following reasons: (1) The associations are geared by law and tradition to local lending;[10] (2) local demand in most areas has been sufficient to absorb the increase in local savings attracted by the generous rate paid on accounts; (3) associations are permitted a high loan-to-value ratio on conventional loans (up to 90

Table 3-8. Mortgage Loans Held by Savings and Loan Associations, at Year End, 1950–1968, Billions of Dollars

	1950	1955	1960	1965	1968
Residential:					
1–4-family	$13.1	$30.0	$55.4	$ 94.2	$110.3
Multifamily	0.3	0.8	2.9	7.6	10.6
	$13.4	$30.8	$58.3	$101.8	$120.9
Commercial and other	0.2	0.5	1.8	8.5	9.9
	$13.6	$31.3	$60.1	$110.3	$130.8
Conventional	$ 9.8	$23.9	$49.3	$ 98.8	$117.1
FHA-insured	0.8	1.4	3.5	5.1	6.7
VA-guaranteed	3.0	6.0	7.2	6.4	7.0
Total	$13.6	$31.3	$60.1	$110.3	$130.8

Sources: *Federal Reserve Bulletin;* United States Savings and Loan League, *Savings and Loan Fact Book* (annual).

[10]In May 1964, the Federal Home Loan Bank Board ruled that Federal associations could write loans up to 5 per cent of assets as far as 100 miles from the regular lending area.

per cent on some categories);[11] (4) the associations make a practice of holding their mortgages to maturity.

Preference for conventional loans is revealed by the relatively small volume of FHA-insured loans held (under 5 per cent of total mortgages in 1968). By and large, associations have not been greatly interested in FHA-type liens for several reasons: (1) dislike of the technicalities of FHA-loan acquisition and reporting; (2) the higher yields available on conventional loans; and (3) their general lack of support of the FHA program because it has attracted other financial institutions into the mortgage field. The aversion to Federally underwritten mortgages has also extended to the VA-guaranteed mortgages, which, at the end of 1968, amounted to $7.0 billions, or 5.4 per cent of mortgage assets. Associations owned 21 per cent of VA loans then outstanding.

Associations have steadily increased their share of total home financing. In 1968, they held $110 billions, or 44 per cent, of the national total of $251 billions of loans on 1–4-family dwellings. The industry is committed to the concept of asset growth, which follows home ownership in its upward trend.

Loans on multifamily structures and on commercial and industrial properties have played an increasing role in recent years, reflecting a search for diversification and higher income. Their importance varies within the industry. A higher proportion in these less stable liens should be offset by higher reserves. Associations offering the highest rate to savers (5 per cent in some cases in the West) must earn a gross rate of close to 7 per cent in order to meet normal operating costs. To earn such a rate the associations must resist the temptation to lower quality standards or to place a high assessed valuation on property in order to support a standard loan-to-property ratio.

Lending authority has recently broadened considerably to include loans for acquisition and development of residential land, for participation in mortgages held by other institutions, and for home improvements. In 1968, the breakdown of loans made, by purpose, was $5.9 billions, or 25 per cent, for home construction; $11.6 billions, or 49 per cent, for home purchases; and $6.1 billions, or 26 per cent, for all other purposes, including multifamily housing and construction loans.[12]

Other Investments

Federally chartered associations may invest in qualified mortgages, Federal securities, obligations of certain Federal agencies, and (since 1964) the four top grades of state and municipal bonds. Treasury bonds are held for liquidity; their proportion to total assets has been in the neighborhood of 6 per cent for several years. The emphasis is on short-

---

[11]For the lending powers of Federal- and state-chartered associations, see Kendall, *The Savings and Loan Business*, pp. 24–27, 158–64.

[12]United States Savings and Loan League, *Savings and Loan Fact Book* (1969), p. 90.

and intermediate-term maturities to reduce price risk and to offset the long maturities of the mortgage portfolio. At the end of 1968, over 60 per cent of Federal bonds held had maturities of 5 years or less.[13] Associations entered the postwar period owning $2.4 billions of United States bonds. In the following 5 years, they liquidated $1 billion to invest in mortgages. At the end of 1968, they owned $9.6 billions of Federal obligations, less than 3 per cent of total Federal securities outstanding. Associations are much less influential in the Federal bond market than are any other major financial institution. The qualified investments of state-chartered associations differ among the states but in general include the types held by the Federals.

Annual Uses of Funds in the Capital Market

Annual data on long-term uses of funds for 1960 through 1968 are shown in Table 3-9.

Comparison with the annual sources-of-funds data on p. 40 shows that the investment in mortgages from 1961 through 1966 exceeded the new savings inflow, resulting in borrowing from the Federal Home Loan Banks.

The rate of acquisition of new home mortgage loans fell off sharply from 1964 through 1966, especially in the latter year, reflecting the decline in institutional savings, the drop in housing starts, and the rise in mortgage interest rates in a period of tightening money. In 1967, a year of monetary ease, there was a sharp recovery in lending volume, but the total still lagged far behind the early 1960's. In 1968, the recovery continued; through 1969, however, not enough savings funds

Table 3-9. Annual Investments in Capital-Market Assets, Savings Associations, 1960–1968, Billions of Dollars

	1960	1961	1962	1963	1964	1965	1966	1967	1968
U.S. government securities	$0.1	$0.6	$ 0.4	$ 0.9	$ 0.5	$0.5	$0.4	$1.5	$0.3
Federal agency securities	—	—	−0.1	0.1	0.1	0.1	0.1	0.3	0.3
Home mortgages	5.9	7.0	7.4	9.3	8.0	7.0	3.1	5.8	6.8
Other mortgages	1.1	1.8	2.6	2.8	2.5	2.0	0.9	1.7	2.2
Total	$7.1	$9.4	$10.3	$13.1	$11.1	$9.6	$4.6	$9.3	$9.6

Sources: Federal Home Loan Bank Board; United States Savings and Loan League, *Savings and Loan Fact Book* (annual). Some columns do not add to totals because of rounding.

[13]*Federal Reserve Bulletin.*

were available to supply the demand for mortgage money, and yields continued to rise. Multifamily and commercial mortgages increased substantially from 1960 through 1963 but gave way to home mortgages in 1964 through 1966. In 1967 and 1968, they enjoyed a sharp rebound, as the increased flow of funds was devoted to higher-yielding mortgages. In 1969 the decline in net savings capital of associations was not reflected in a similar decline in the rate of growth of mortgage holdings, which increased $7.8 billions in the first 9 months. Much of this increase was financed by reductions in liquid assets and by borrowing from the Federal Home Loan Banks.

Additions to Federal securities change with the varying need for liquidity and the demand for mortgage loans.

Influence of Monetary Policy

Savings and loan associations specialize in mortgage assets with original long maturities. Their average portfolio maturity is from 8 to 12 years, reflecting steady amortization. Once committed, the rate earned on a mortgage remains unchanged. Similarly, rates paid to savers, the same to both new and old, change only at intervals that may be months apart, or even a year or two. As a result, variations in market rates resulting from tighter or easier Federal Reserve policy affect only new lending activity, and the associations earn and pay rates whose changes lag behind open-market yields. Nevertheless, such changes affect the volume of new housing starts and new mortgage commitments. Associations also feel the influence of capital-market forces through the availability and cost of advances from the Federal Home Loan Banks, which in turn must obtain their own funds at open-market yields.

Role in a National Mortgage Market

Savings and loan associations operate mainly at home. Unlike other lenders—mutual savings banks and life insurance companies in particular—they have used agents or correspondents to originate and service their loans to only a minor extent.

Associations do, however, contribute to a national flow of funds in several ways. First, they purchase and sell mortgages from other associations, commercial banks, insurance companies, mortgage companies, and brokers, and they participate with each other and with other lenders in large loans. In 1968, insured associations purchased $2.3 billions of loans and participations and sold $690 millions. The difference of $1.6 billions represents net purchases outside the industry.[14] Second, by borrowing from Federal Home Loan Banks, associations tap national sources of capital for local employment. Third, savings funds are attracted

---

[14]United States Savings and Loan League, *Savings and Loan Fact Book* (1969), p. 91.

from out-of-town areas where yields on deposit investments are lower. California associations aggressively advertise to attract funds by offering the highest yields on a national basis. The fact that most accounts are insured (to $15,000) by the Federal Savings and Loan Insurance Corporation is a major factor in inducing investors to shift funds to distant associations.

Savings and loan associations as a group are not active in the general secondary-mortgage market. They have used the Federal National Mortgage Association as a market but to a much lesser extent than other institutions, mainly because the association deals in FHA-insured and VA-guaranteed liens only.

```
44444444444444444444444444444444444444444444444444444444444444444444444444444444
44444444444444444444444444444444444444444444444444444444444444444444444444444444
44444444444444444444444444444444    444    444444444444    444444444444444444444444444444
44444444444444444444444444444444    4444    4444444444    444444444444444444444444444444
44444444444444444444444444444444    44444    444444444    444444444444444444444444444444
44444444444444444444444444444444    444444    4444444    444444444444444444444444444444
44444444444444444444444444444444    4444444    44444    444444444444444444444444444444
44444444444444444444444444444444    44444444    444    444444444444444444444444444444
44444444444444444444444444444444    444444444    4    444444444444444444444444444444
44444444444444444444444444444444    444444444        444444444444444444444444444444
44444444444444444444444444444444    4444444444        444444444444444444444444444444
44444444444444444444444444444444444444444444444444444444444444444444444444444444
44444444444444444444444444444444444444444444444444444444444444444444444444444444
```

Insurance Companies

IN this chapter we deal with the two major insurance institutions: legal reserve life insurance companies and property and liability companies. The two perform quite distinct functions. They draw on different sources of funds, and their uses of funds affect somewhat different segments of the capital market.

Life Insurance Companies

Nature and Functions

Life insurance companies are the largest single medium for individual savings in the United States. Their total assets have grown from $64 billions in 1950 to $189 billions at the end of 1968 and consist chiefly of a variety of capital-market instruments from which no important category is omitted. The annual rate of asset growth now exceeds $10 billions, or 6 per cent.

Life insurance companies provide financial protection for beneficiaries against death and longevity (life insurance and annuities). They can, however, be classed as financial intermediaries. In policies other than renewable term and industrial, the level premium includes a reserve or savings element that represents an amount in excess of need for current death losses. This is invested and compounded to cover death losses at later ages. The level annual premiums on annuities include amounts accumulated to provide a life income based on actuarial life expectancy.

Thus, life insurance companies perform two major functions: (1) protection of beneficiaries against premature death (insurance) and unusual longevity (annuities) of the policyholders; and (2) investment of funds representing policy reserves (and other funds) in a wide variety of capital-market instruments.

General Relation to the Capital Market

Because the contracts of life insurance companies involve, for the most part, long-term liabilities, the savings they accumulate are placed mainly in capital-market rather than money-market instruments. Except for those held for liquidity purposes, the securities and mortgages in the investment portfolio are ordinarily held to maturity as long as they meet required standards of quality. Investment policy emphasizes long-term safety and the achievement of a return that produces the rates built into premium calculations at which reserves must be compounded.

At the end of 1968 about $163 billions, or 85 per cent, of the total assets of life insurance companies consisted of Federal, state, and municipal bonds; corporate and foreign bonds; mortgages; and corporate stock. Capital-market investments grow at about $6 to $8 billions each year. The net premium and investment income, plus funds from maturing bonds and mortgages, provides an annual cash flow of $18 to $20 billions. The policies of the industry with respect to the purchase and sale of various classes of assets are a very potent factor in the capital markets.

Sources of Funds

The major source of external funds is the accumulating reserve liabilities derived from net premium income and the compounding of investment income. Between 1950 and 1968, policy reserves grew from $55 to $154 billions. Accumulated policy "dividends" (rebates), reserves for future dividends, and other obligations provide additional funds. The total of these last 3 sources grew from $5 to $21 billions in the same period. Net worth accounts, including special and unassigned surplus and the capital stock accounts of stock companies, increased from $5 to $17 billions. Most of these sources represent long-term obligations, so capital-market assets are appropriate investments.

The annual sources of new funds for capital-market use from 1960 through 1968 are derived by deducting from the annual increase in total assets the changes in miscellaneous assets, net cash, real estate, and policy loans (billions of dollars):[1]

1960	1961	1962	1963	1964	1965	1966	1967	1968
$4.6	$5.3	$5.7	$6.1	$7.0	$7.7	$6.6	$7.5	$7.2

Cash flow from sale of securities and maturing mortgages, totaling about $10 billions, was also available for reinvestment annually in recent years.

Factors Determining General Investment Policy

Before examining actual investment policy, we should note the major factors stemming from the nature of the business and its regulation that determine the general character of the investments.

(1) Contracts with policyholders are essentially long-term obligations. Although some mature every day, the cash drain can be forecast with considerable accuracy, as can the cash inflow from net new premiums, the maturing and sales of securities and mortgages, and investment income. Most life insurance contracts provide for an accumulation of cash surrender values payable or loaned on demand. However, experience with policy loans and liquidation of cash values shows that only under extreme conditions (as during the early 1930's) are large permanent withdrawals likely to occur. And for the growing insurance company, steady cash inflow more than exceeds the cash drain for death benefits, expenses, and withdrawals.

The emphasis can therefore be placed on acquisition of long-maturity instruments, and the general practice is to hold these to maturity, unless changes in market yields cause shifts in broad categories of investments or unless a loss of quality of individual investments requires their liquidation.

(2) Some liquidity is, however, required to provide for day-to-day needs, to meet large emergency death losses, and to permit changes among investment categories without sudden sale of assets. Liquidity is provided by working cash balances, Federal bonds, and amortization of mortgages and loans.

(3) Premiums are written on the assumption of a minimum rate of return at which funds representing reserves will be compounded (e.g., 3 to $3\frac{1}{2}$ per cent). A steady and adequate yield is therefore required. Investment policy must emphasize fixed-income assets of high quality and stable income. It is also desirable to earn a rate of return in excess of the "guaranteed" rate and so distribute premium rebates in "dividends."

(4) Their position as trustees of savings requires that life insurance companies invest funds for ultimate safety. This is achieved by restrict-

[1]Source: Institute of Life Insurance, *Life Insurance Fact Book* (annual).

ing investments to instruments that meet the standards of quality established by policy and regulation. Diversification by type of investment, industrial category, maturity, and degree of marketability is also a means of protecting against losses of principal.

(5) Actuarial commitments require insurance companies to remain fully invested, keeping cash balance to the minimum set by estimated cash inflows and outflows. This requirement explains the use of forward commitments for business loans and mortgages; it also explains the use of mortgage company correspondents to originate and service mortgages in capital-seeking areas to which surplus funds can be directed (see Chapter 11).

(6) Valuation of assets for statement purposes has a considerable effect on investment policy. Mutual companies are permitted to build up only limited surplus accounts, and competition prevents stock companies from accumulating large excess premium deposits. Substantial declines in assets values must therefore be avoided. Quality must be emphasized, and bond accounts so managed as to prevent large write-downs of assets because of shifts in market rates of interest.

(7) Life insurance income is not tax free, although the Federal income-tax rate is substantially less than that applying to business corporations. The increase in the effective rate in 1959 (from 7–8 per cent to 21–22 per cent) has led to greater interest in the obligations of state and local governments.

(8) Because commitments are in fixed dollars, little attention need be paid to actual or potential inflation. Rising operating costs can be met by gradual changes in premiums. Common stocks and real estate are acquired more for their greater long-run income than for their value as inflation hedges.

(9) The effect of state regulation of life insurance investments is important enough to warrant special discussion.

Regulation

In all 50 states, the investments of life insurance companies are heavily affected by regulation specifying the categories of investments that can be acquired and the standards of quality that each permitted category must meet.[2] Companies domiciled in one state and doing business in others must conform to the standards required of domestic insurers insofar as locally generated reserves are concerned, as well as those of the state of domicile. Corporate bonds must meet standards as to type and value of collateral or interest coverage or both; the latter requirement is stricter for unsecured obligations. Conventional mort-

---

[2] For a convenient discussion of regulation and a summary of the specific regulations in 19 representative states, see Life Insurance Association of America, *Life Insurance Companies as Financial Institutions,* a monograph prepared for the Commission on Money and Credit (Englewood Cliffs, N.J.: Prentice-Hall, Inc., 1962), Chap. 5 and Appendix.

gages must meet maximum loan-to-appraised-value ratios (as high as 75 per cent on 1- or 2-family dwellings in New York and some other states). Preferred stocks must meet specified tests of dividend coverage and payment. Common stocks, now permitted in limited amounts in the majority of states, must ordinarily be listed and meet specified earnings and dividend tests. Income-producing real estate is restricted as to type and use of property.

The individual states establish what percentage each category of investments may be of total assets and also restrict the percentages of assets invested in the obligations of one (private) borrower. Geographic limitations on investments also apply, as do requirements in a few states that a certain percentage of reserves be invested in instruments originating in that state. Fortunately, the latter requirement is not widespread; it would prevent companies from directing their funds to the areas of greatest need and best yields.

Actual Investment Policy

Table 4-1 shows the combined assets and percentages of legal reserve companies by major categories from 1950 through 1968 (at year end).

United States government securities   In 1945, these obligations totaled $20.6 billions, or 46 per cent of total assets. Treasury obligations have since declined in both amount and percentage and, at the end of 1968, totaled $4.4 billions, or only 2.4 per cent of total assets. During the decade of sharpest decline—1945 through 1955—the annual shrinkage averaged $1.2 billions. Treasury obligations are held for liquidity and diversification and as a residual source of funds for other use.

The big shift has been into corporate bonds and mortgages. The relative yields were greatly affected by the accord between the Treasury and the Federal Reserve banks in 1951, when the prices and yields of Treasury securities were "unpegged" (see Chapter 7). The massive sales of insurance companies (along with those of other institutions) of Treasury obligations were an important factor leading to the accord. In the later 1950's and the 1960's, net sales of these securities continued at a varying pace depending on the availability of and yields on alternative investments.

At the end of 1968, the $4.4 billions of Federal securities represented 1.2 per cent of total Federal debt and 1.9 per cent of marketable Federal obligations. The emphasis has been on intermediate- and long-term maturities. In 1968, only $320 millions were in Treasury bills and certificates.

State and local government bonds   The increase in holdings of American state and local government bonds, from $1.1 billions, or 1.7 per cent of total assets, in 1950 to $3.2 billions, or 1.6 per cent, at the end of 1968 reflected two main factors: (1) the attractive yields on these bonds that in turn reflected the postwar increase in state and local

Table 4-1. Combined Assets of Legal Reserve Life Insurance Companies, Amounts and Percentages, at Year End, 1950–1968, Billions of Dollars

	1950	Per Cent	1955	Per Cent	1960	Per Cent	1965	Per Cent	1968	Per Cent
U.S. government securities	$13.5	21.1	$8.6	9.5	$6.4	5.4	$5.1	3.2	$4.4	2.4
Federal agency securities	—	—	—	—	0.1	—	0.2	0.1	0.4	0.2
American municipal bonds	1.1	1.7	2.0	2.2	3.6	3.0	3.5	2.2	3.2	1.6
Canadian municipal bonds	0.4	0.6	0.7	0.8	1.0	0.8	1.9	1.2	2.2	1.1
Foreign central government bonds	1.0	1.6	0.4	0.4	0.4	0.3	0.9	0.6	0.7	0.4
Corporate bonds	23.4	36.6	36.1	39.9	47.0	39.4	58.6	37.0	68.5	36.3
Mortgages	16.1	25.1	29.4	32.5	41.8	35.0	60.0	37.8	70.0	37.2
Preferred stocks	1.5	2.3	1.7	1.9	1.8	1.5	2.9	1.9	3.2	1.6
Common stocks	0.6	1.0	1.9	2.1	3.2	2.7	6.2	3.8	10.0	5.3
Policy loans	2.4	3.7	3.3	3.7	5.2	4.3	7.7	4.8	11.3	6.0
Real estate	1.4	2.2	2.6	2.9	3.8	3.2	4.7	3.0	5.6	3.0
Cash and other assets	2.6	4.1	3.7	4.1	5.3	4.4	7.2	4.5	9.1	4.9
Total assets	$64.0	100	$90.4	100	$119.6	100	$158.9	100	$188.6	100

Source: Institute of Life Insurance, *Life Insurance Fact Book* (annual).

borrowing (see Chapter 8); and (2) the substantial increase in federal income-tax rates on insurance companies since 1958. Such bonds are also acquired for general portfolio diversification. However, both the dollar amount and the relative amount of American "municipals" have decreased substantially since 1960. The tax-exempt feature is less attractive to companies not in a high bracket when yields on corporate bonds and mortgages are very high and when appreciation is sought through investment in equities.

General obligations of state and local governments do not have as much appeal to insurance companies as revenue bonds, which enjoy income-tax exemption yet sell at yields often equal to those on fully taxable good and high-grade corporate bonds and also provide generally long maturities. At the end of 1968, revenue bonds constituted 70 per cent of insurance company holdings of American municipal bonds.

Life insurance companies' share of American state and municipal long-term securities has changed from 4.3 per cent of the $23 billions outstanding in 1950 to 3.1 per cent of the $104 billions outstanding at the end of 1968.

Corporate bonds   One of the most important features of insurance company investments since World War II has been the increase in corporate bond holdings. In 1945, these totaled $10.1 billions and constituted 22.5 per cent of total assets; they increased to $68.5 billions and 36.3 per cent of assets by the end of 1968. They have constituted 36 to 40 per cent of total assets in the 1950's and 1960's. The funds for this expansion were provided in the early years by the switch from United States government bonds and later by the great growth of net cash flow.

Corporate bonds are attractive to insurance companies because of their superior yield, quoted prices (save for those acquired through private placement), marketability, and variety. Along with its absolute and relative growth, the composition of the bond portfolio has undergone a marked change. The waning investment status of railway bonds led to the decline in their percentage of total assets from 4.9 per cent ($3.3 billions) in 1950 to 1.9 per cent ($3.6 billions) in 1968. At the same time, there was a substantial increase in utility bond holdings, which grew from $10.6 billions, or 16.5 per cent of total assets, in 1950 to $17.6 billions, or 9.3 per cent, in 1968. This growth reflected the burgeoning postwar expansion of the utility industries, especially gas and electric power, and their improved investment status. (However, such bonds have become relatively less attractive in recent years because of their low yields and because they are usually issued through competitive bidding, in which insurance companies seldom participate.)

The industrial bond category has shown a remarkable growth—from $9.5 billions, or 1.9 per cent of assets, in 1950 to $47.8 billions, or 25.5 per cent, in 1968. This growth reflects the upgrading of the investment status of industrial obligations—especially in such rapidly growing fields as oil, chemicals, and finance—and the fact that the great bulk of high-grade issues are acquired through direct placement, in which life insurance companies play the leading role (see Chapter 9). The industrial bond category also includes long-term loans similar to, but with longer maturities than, bank term loans.

The life insurance industry is extremely important in the corporate bond market. Net investment in these assets increased by $45 billions from 1950 through 1968. At the end of 1968, insurance companies owned 44 per cent of all corporate bonds outstanding.

Mortgages   The large holdings of mortgages of the life insurance industry (see Table 4-2) reflect the following characteristics of these assets: (1) relatively attractive yields (1 to 2 per cent above high-grade bonds); (2) ultimate safety as required by strict regulation; (3) long maturities; (4) steady amortization of principal, which contributes

Table 4-2.   Mortgage Loans Held by Legal Reserve Life Insurance
Companies, at Year End, 1950–1968, Billions of Dollars

	1950	1955	1960	1965	1968
Farm	$ 1.3	$ 2.3	$ 3.0	$ 4.8	$ 5.8
Residential:					
1–4-family	8.5	17.7	24.9	29.9	29.6
Multifamily	2.6	3.5	3.9	8.4	12.8
	$11.1	$21.2	$28.8	$38.3	$42.4
Commercial and other	3.7	5.9	10.0	16.9	21.8
Total	$16.1	$29.4	$41.8	$60.0	$70.0
Conventional and other	$ 9.5	$16.9	$25.8	$41.6	$52.0
FHA-insured (nonfarm)	4.6	6.4	9.0	12.1	12.0
VA-guaranteed	2.0	6.1	6.9	6.3	6.0
Total	$16.1	$29.4	$41.8	$60.0	$70.0

Sources: *Federal Reserve Bulletin*; Institute of Life Insurance, *Life Insurance Fact Book* (annual); United States Savings and Loan League, *Savings and Loan Fact Book* (annual); Federal Home Loan Bank Board, *Savings and Home Finance Source Book* (annual).

greatly to liquidity; (5) growing geographical diversification through the use of the mortgage correspondent and wider-spread direct investment; (6) growing diversity of types; (7) the special appeal of FHA-insured and VA-guaranteed loans; and (8) loan-to-value ratios on conventional residential liens as high as 75 per cent in some states. These advantages are somewhat offset by the costlier management and poorer marketability of mortgage investments as compared with listed securities.

Mortgage investments have increased in each postwar year in both amount and percentage of total assets, rising from $16.1 billions, or 25 per cent of total assets, in 1950 to $70.0 billions, or 37 per cent of assets, at the end of 1968—an average increase of $3 billions per year. Such growth reflects both the general expansion of mortgage financing in the postwar period and the larger share of the total held by the industry.

At the end of 1968, loans on 1–4-family residential properties totaling $29.6 billions constituted 42 per cent of mortgage holdings and 16 per cent of total assets. FHA-insured and VA-guaranteed loans fell from 41 per cent of mortgage assets in 1950 to 25 per cent in 1968, when they totaled $18 billions, or about 10 per cent of assets. This was nearly one-quarter of the total outstanding. The preference of many companies for conventional residential loans partly explains why the total of this latter category accounted for 28 per cent of assets in 1968.

The annual investment in residential mortgages has been by no means regular but has followed cyclical rises and falls in housing starts (for example, large increases in 1953 through 1956, 1959, 1960, 1963, and 1964, and decreases in 1968 and 1969). Mortgages in general compete mainly with bonds, and each major category of mortgages also competes with other types. The ebb and flow of funds into Federally supported mortgages has also been irregular, varying with relative interest rates on competitive investments. The investment in these Federally underwritten loans has seen the most variation because their nominal interest rates are pegged and are changed only at rather long intervals. Life insurance companies have not been enthusiastic about buying such investments at a discount when the nominal rate is inadequate (see Chapter 11).

As a group, life insurance companies are the second most important institutional owner of residential mortgages, surpassed by only savings and loan associations (see Chapters 3, 11). At the end of 1968, life insurance companies held 12 per cent of outstanding loans on 1–4-family residences.

The flow of funds into home mortgages became negative in 1968 and 1969 for a variety of reasons: the decline in housing starts; the increase in policy loans made at low rates of interest that forced a search for higher-yielding investments; and the greater attraction of commercial and industrial mortgages which not only produced higher yields (up to 9 per cent in 1969) but provided equity participation or other "kickers" such as a share in gross or net income above a fixed minimum.

Because of their great resources and large staffs, larger insurance companies are greatly interested in mortgages on multifamily and commercial properties for both diversification and higher income. The holdings of this industry of these mortgages increased to $34.6 billions, or 18 per cent of total assets, at the end of 1968. Included in the commercial category are some term loans for business purposes. At the end of 1968, insurance companies held 27 per cent of multifamily and 30 per cent of commercial real estate loans outstanding.

Farm mortgage investments totaled $5.8 billions at the end of 1968, or 3 per cent of total assets. This percentage has remained fairly static in recent years but is related to a steady increase in dollar amount. The industry is the largest institutional owner of such liens, holding 23 per cent of the national total at the end of 1968.

Life insurance companies rely heavily on local mortgage correspondents for the origination of their mortgage loans, especially residential liens (see Chapter 11). Over 40 per cent of their total mortgages and about two-thirds of their single-family home-mortgage loans were obtained in this fashion in 1967. Reliance on mortgage companies declined in 1968 and 1969 with the decrease in home financing. (The contribution of mortgage companies to a growing national market in mortgages and to greater geographical uniformity in interest rates is indicated in Chapter 11.)

Corporate stocks   Certain reasons for the traditional lack of interest in common stocks have already been indicated, including the need of steady and secure income and of safety of principal and the lack of need of inflation in hedging. Tradition, law (restricting common stock investment to a small percentage of assets or of policyholders' surplus and limiting the amount of investment in any one company), and the required valuation at year-end market price also discourage greater holdings of this asset.

Holdings of common stocks have, however, increased in amount, and have steadily increased in percentage of total assets for several years. In 1968, the total was $10 billions, or 5.3 per cent, with emphasis on solid blue chips. These figures reflect the appreciation in appraised value. Preferred stocks, whose appeal is for current income, totaled $3.2 billions, or 1.6 per cent of total assets.

The interest of life insurance companies in common stocks is likely to increase substantially in the future. Indirect interest derives from participation in the operation of mutual (open-end) investment funds. Direct interest reflects the mounting importance of insured pension plans invested in equities, with the portfolios segregated from general assets, and the relaxation of state rules to permit a higher proportion of life insurance reserves to be invested in equities.

Although $10 billions is no small amount, it suggests that the influence of this institution in the stock market lags far behind that of others. At the end of 1968, insurance companies owned 1.3 per cent of the value of stocks listed on the New York Stock Exchange.[3]

Annual Uses of Funds

The annual capital-market uses of life insurance company funds

Table 4-3.   Annual Changes in Capital-Market Assets, Life Insurance Companies, 1960–1968, Billions of Dollars

	1960	1961	1962	1963	1964	1965	1966	1967	1968
U.S. government securities	$—0.4	$—0.3	$—	$—0.4	$—0.2	$—0.5	$—0.3	$—0.2	$—0.2
State and local government bonds	0.4	0.3	0.1	—0.2	—0.1	—0.2	—0.4	—0.1	—
Foreign securities	0.3	0.5	0.7	0.8	0.4	0.4	0.2	0.2	0.1
Corporate bonds	1.4	2.0	1.8	2.1	1.9	2.4	2.2	3.7	3.6
Corporate stocks	0.4	0.4	0.4	0.2	0.4	0.7	0.3	1.0	1.2
Home mortgages	1.3	0.9	0.6	0.8	1.4	1.2	0.5	—0.5	—0.2
Other mortgages	1.3	1.5	2.1	2.8	3.2	3.7	4.1	3.4	2.7
Total	$4.6	$5.3	$5.7	$6.1	$7.0	$7.7	$6.6	$7.5	$7.2

Source: Institute of Life Insurance, *Life Insurance Fact Book*. Common stocks data are net of changes in market value. Some columns do not add to total because of rounding.

[3]New York Stock Exchange, *Fact Book, 1969,* p. 45.

from 1955 through 1968 are shown in Table 4-3. The influences indicated earlier in this chapter are clearly revealed by these data: the selloff of Federal bonds, the steady accumulation of corporate bonds, the varying rate of net acquisition of home mortgages, and the increase in commercial and multifamily liens. During the tight money year of 1966, liquidation of public securities provided funds for continued acquisition of corporate bonds and commercial mortgages, while net purchases of home mortgages declined substantially. This trend continued through 1967. In 1968, the total supply of new funds declined, and there was again a net disinvestment in home mortgages and a decline in the rate of acquisition of other mortgages. Net investment in corporate stocks increased to a new high. The year 1969 saw a continuation of these tendencies.

From 1961 through 1968, corporate bonds accounted for nearly 40 per cent of the increase in capital-market assets, and all mortgages for 53 per cent.

Influence in the National Capital Markets

Life insurance companies direct between $18 and $20 billions of new and internal funds into the capital markets each year. They are the dominating force, on the demand side, for corporate bonds and are second only to savings and loan associations in the mortgage market. Their decisions concerning investment of this great stream of capital greatly affect yields in some markets. Likewise, changes in market yields influence the direction of their funds toward different categories of assets.

In the later 1960's, the movement toward all-purpose financial combines included the acquisition, by a number of life insurance companies or their parents, of mutual fund management companies, mortgage banking firms, and property insurers. The consolidated statements of such groups lose the characteristics of those of insurance companies, and their flows of funds become less and less typical of the life insurance industry as such.

Property and Liability Insurance Companies

Nature and Scope of Industry

The property-liability insurance group contains over 4,000 companies (1969) with assets in excess of $50 billions consisting mainly of capital-market securities. Unlike life insurance companies, property and liability companies do not collect savings. They sell a service, and their liabilities do not represent firm dollar obligations to policyholders. They acquire their assets almost exclusively in the secondary markets.

Their aggregate resources include a very respectable percentage of outstanding government and corporate instruments, and so investment policies exert an important influence on the market for outstanding long-term securities. Although our discussion, in the main, pertains to the whole industry, two important subclassifications should be recognized: (1) mutual and stock companies; (2) insurers of property loss due to fire, etc., and insurers of personal liability.

Mutual companies do not issue stock but are owned by their policyholders. Their net worth is appropriately called "policyholders' surplus." The net worth of stock companies (capital stock and surplus) also constitutes protection to policyholders and so is also called policyholders' surplus, using the term in a broad sense. The distinction between the two types of ownership has an important influence on investment policy.

Insurers against loss to property from fire and other causes sell contracts that provide for indemnification of damage losses up to the limits of the policy. The actual losses depend on the cost of repair or replacement. Casualty insurance companies (auto, workmen's compensation, etc.) are primarily concerned with losses caused by injuries to persons and by damage to property of others. Many casualty companies also write fidelity and surety insurance.

"Multiple-line" companies, offering a variety of lines of property or casualty insurance or both are found in both the mutual and stock categories.

Two minor types of organizations are *reciprocal exchanges*—cooperatives formed to provide coverage for members at cost—and *domestic Lloyds*—associations of unincorporated individuals that underwrite unusual risks.

Sources of Funds

Investment funds are derived mainly from (1) premium income allocated to two types of reserves for possible payment to policyholders: reserve for losses and reserve for unearned premiums; (2) increases in policyholders' surplus consisting of capital (stock) and surplus and voluntary reserves of stock companies; and guarantee funds, net surplus, and voluntary reserves of mutuals. Loss reserves represent liability for claims that have been filed and that are anticipated (a 60 to 65 per cent loss ratio is assumed). Premiums are collected in advance and are not fully earned until the policies expire (1, 3, or 5 years for fire, 1 year for casualty), and so the unearned premium reserve represents the amount that would be returned to policyholders for the unexpired terms if all policies were canceled.

The actual net worth of a company is higher than reported because part of the unearned premium reserve represents funds in excess of actual need. Acquisition costs have already been incurred, and the risks could be reinsured for less than the prepaid premium. Analysts transfer 35 to 40 per cent of this reserve in calculating adjusted actual net worth.

The distinction between reserves and policyholders' surplus is important in determining investment policy. The data in Table 4-4 show the amounts and relative proportions of these accounts, along with total assets, from 1950 through 1968. (Net worth is unadjusted.) The data exclude reciprocal and domestic Lloyds companies and represent about 97 per cent of the industry in the United States.

For both types of companies, the relative size of policyholders' surplus compared with reserves has steadily increased, reaching 37 per cent of total assets in 1968, compared with 55 per cent provided by reserves. This cushion against decline in asset values and calamitous losses has been consistently greater for stock companies than for mutuals.

Annual Sources of Funds, 1960–1968

The annual sources of new funds from 1960 through 1968 are shown in Table 4-5. The decline in unearned premium reserve accumulation in certain years reflects unfavorable loss experience. After deducting

Table 4-4. Reserves and Net Worth, Property-Liability Insurance Companies, 1950–1968, Billions of Dollars

	1950	1955	1960	1965	1968
Loss reserves:					
Stock companies	$ 3.6	$ 3.4	$ 5.4	$ 8.7	$10.9
Mutuals	0.7	1.3	2.1	3.4	4.3
	$ 4.3	$ 4.7	$ 7.5	$12.1	$15.2
Unearned premium reserves:					
Stock companies	2.5	5.1	6.6	8.3	9.5
Mutuals	0.7	1.1	1.6	2.3	2.5
	$3.2	$ 6.2	$ 8.2	$10.6	$12.0
Policyholders' surplus:					
Stock companies	4.2	7.7	9.5	13.7	14.9
Mutuals	1.0	1.6	2.1	3.1	3.4
	$ 5.2	$ 9.3	$11.6	$16.8	$18.3
Total reserves and net worth	$12.7	$20.2	$27.3	$39.5	$45.5
Total assets:					
Stock companies	$10.6	$17.3	$22.8	$31.3	$37.7
Mutuals	2.5	4.5	6.6	9.4	11.5
	$13.1	$21.8	$29.4	$40.7	$49.2

Source: Alfred M. Best Co., Inc., *Best's Aggregates and Averages, Property-Liability* (annual).

the annual changes in cash and miscellaneous assets from the figures in Table 4-5, the following sums were available for capital-market use (billions of dollars):

1960	1961	1962	1963	1964	1965	1966	1967	1968
$1.2	$1.3	$1.2	$1.3	$1.1	$0.9	$1.6	$2.2	$2.8 (est.)

Differences among sources of funds play an important part in investment policy. Reserve liabilities have short and intermediate maturity, depending on the length of policies (1 to 5 years). If an insurance company were to stop writing new business, it would pay out on existing claims approximately the amount of its loss reserves plus that portion of unearned premium credited to loss reserves as the policies neared expiration. This payment coverage would require extreme liquidity. Actually, however, most companies can meet both expenses and losses from new premium income. This income relieves the pressure for liquidity, but it does not remove the price risk on portfolio. The possible need to sell securities in large amounts to meet calamitous losses requires not only a thick equity cushion, but also limited vulnerability to fluctuations in the market value of portfolio assets.

Uses of Funds

Two major functions are performed: underwriting of risk and investment of funds in a diversified portfolio of securities. The two are, however, closely related. The substantial holdings of Federal securities and other high-grade assets reflect the obligation of the companies to meet all underwritten losses when incurred. Unlike life insurance companies, fire and casualty companies are unable to estimate future claims with actuarial accuracy.

Table 4-5.   Sources of Funds, Property-Liability Insurance Companies, 1960–1968, Billions of Dollars

	1960	1961	1962	1963	1964	1965	1966	1967	1968*
Unearned premium reserves	$0.3	$0.1	$0.3	$0.5	$0.4	$0.6	$0.7	$0.7	$0.8
Loss reserves	0.7	0.6	0.6	0.7	0.9	1.0	1.2	1.4	1.5
Policyholders' surplus	0.3	0.7	0.7	0.4	0.2	−0.3	0.4	0.6	0.5
Total	$1.4	$1.5	$1.5	$1.5	$1.6	$1.3	$2.2	$2.7	$2.8

*Estimated.
Sources: Best Co., Inc., *Best's Aggregates and Averages, Property-Liability*; Bankers Trust Company, *The Investment Outlook* (annual). Policyholders' surplus is net of changes in market values of assets. Certain columns do not add to totals because of rounding.

Table 4-6 shows the combined percentage distribution of the assets of fire and casualty companies from 1950 through 1967.[4] The data conceal substantial variations within the group resulting from factors discussed below.

Factors Affecting Investment Policy

Various factors determine the investment policy of property and liability insurance companies.

Type of organization   Mutual companies lack the investment of stockholders as a cushion against losses in asset values. The policy-holders' surplus belongs to the clients rather than to proprietors. The investment policy of mutual companies is more conservative. Bonds and preferred stock constituted 68 per cent of total assets at the end of 1968. The relative importance of Federal bonds has, however, declined substantially in the postwar period.

Table 4-6.   Combined Assets of Property–Liability Insurance Companies, Amounts and Percentages, at Year End, 1950–1968, Billions of Dollars

	1950	Per Cent	1955	Per Cent	1960	Per Cent	1965	Per Cent	1968	Per Cent
U.S. government securities	$ 5.5	41.0	$ 6.2	28.3	$ 5.8	19.3	$ 6.0	14.4	$ 5.4	10.5
Federal agency securities	—	—	0.1	—	0.2	0.7	0.5	1.2	0.3	0.6
State and local government bonds:										
General	1.1	8.2	3.0	13.5	5.2	17.3	5.7	13.6	7.2	14.1
Revenue	—	—	1.3	5.8	3.0	10.0	5.5	13.2	7.2	14.1
Corporate bonds	0.6	4.5	1.1	5.0	1.7	5.6	2.6	6.2	5.0	9.8
Preferred stock	0.7	5.2	0.9	4.0	0.8	2.7	1.1	2.6	1.4	2.7
Common stock	2.8	20.9	6.0	26.9	8.6	28.6	14.1	33.7	16.7	32.6
Mortgages	0.1	0.8	0.2	1.0	0.1	0.3	0.1	0.2	0.2	0.4
Premium balances	0.9	6.7	1.2	5.4	2.0	6.6	2.6	6.2	3.4	6.6
Cash	1.3	9.7	1.5	6.5	1.4	4.6	1.3	3.1	1.3	2.5
Other assets	0.4	3.0	0.8	3.6	1.3	4.3	2.3	5.5	3.1	6.1
Total	$13.4	100	$22.3	100	$30.1	100	$41.8	100	$51.2	100

Source: Best Co., Inc., *Best's Aggregates and Averages, Property-Liability.*

[4]The total asset figures do not agree with those given on p. 60. The breakdown of the assets of smaller companies is included.

Type of business written Property insurance policies may cover terms as long as 5 years, whereas liability policies typically cover 1 year. Companies writing casualty insurance need greater liquidity.

Regulations for safety and liquidity State laws governing investments vary considerably. In general, they require (1) investment in high-grade bonds of funds representing reserves and *minimum* required policyholders' surplus or capital; (2) adequate diversification; (3) observance of quality standards (for example, for stocks, a certain dividend history).

Sources of funds Ability to meet all claims under any conditions requires avoidance of substantial price risks. Premiums are collected in advance, and funds representing reserves must be available at all times. In 1968, cash plus premium income in process of collection plus bonds equaled 58 per cent of total assets. Loss reserves and unearned premiums represented 50 per cent of total assets.

The proportion of liquid assets has declined in recent years. This decline reflects chiefly the increase in book (year-end market) value of stocks held rather than a deliberate reduction of liquidity.

Tax relief Stock companies pay the corporate income-tax rate on net investment income and net underwriting profits. Mutuals are taxed (since 1962) on substantially the same basis.[5] As a result corporate bonds, with their fully taxable interest, are not in favor. By contrast, tax-exempt direct obligations of state and municipal governments and tax-free revenue bonds constituted 33 per cent of the total assets of mutuals at the end of 1968. Stock companies had a smaller percentage in this asset because of the larger relative importance of common stocks in their portfolios.

Need for inflation protection At the end of 1968, stock companies had 35 per cent and mutuals 18 per cent of total assets in common stocks. Much of the shift to common stock in recent years reflects the need for price appreciation as protection against increasing costs of repair and replacement. In addition, 85 per cent of dividend income is tax exempt. Nevertheless, there is a wide variation in policy; some companies emphasize common stocks, while others own relatively small amounts.

Liquidity Liquidity needs are provided by cash and high-grade bonds. Recently, the main interest in Federal bonds has been in the short- and intermediate-term categories because of their lesser price risk and because their yield is (1969) slightly above those of long maturities (see Chapter 7).

---

[5]Mutual companies are permitted to establish pretax protection against loss accounts in an amount equal to 1 per cent of insurance losses during the year and 25 per cent of ordinary underwriting income for a period of 5 years. Mutual companies that elect to distribute their underwriting profit to policyholders are allowed full deduction for these "dividends."

Volume of business and loss experience   Both rapidly rising volume of premiums written and an adverse record of underwriting losses require a conservative investment policy. The combination of insurance and investment "exposure," together with the other factors mentioned above, sets the pattern for the individual company.

Annual Uses of Funds, 1960–1968

The data in Table 4-7 show the net disposition of funds in capital-market assets in recent years. Federal bonds are not as attractive to property and liability companies as they are to some other institutional investors; these companies need less liquidity and require investment income to offset underwriting losses and to provide earnings for dividends. The major emphasis has been on tax-free state and municipal bonds, save in years like 1964 and 1965, when deficit underwriting operations made nontaxable bonds less attractive. Net acquisitions of corporate stocks (mostly common) have been important but volatile. Corporate bonds remain relatively out of favor, although their very attractive yields did draw some additional funds from 1964 through 1968.

Role in the Capital Market

Property and casualty insurance companies, with $51 billions of assets, of which $43 billions consisted of securities at the end of 1968, form a major segment of the demand for corporate securities. They owned $5.4 billions, or 2.3 per cent, of the marketable Federal debt, $14.4 billions, or 11 per cent, of state and local debt, and $14.8 billions, or 2 per cent, of common stock outstanding. Their role in the corporate bond and mortgage markets is negligible.

Table 4-7.   Net Disposition of Funds in Capital-Market Assets, Property–Liability Insurance Companies, at Year End, 1960–1968, Billions of Dollars

	1960	1961	1962	1963	1964	1965	1966	1967	1968
U.S. government securities	$ —	$ —	$0.1	$ —	$0.1	$ —	$0.2	$—0.8	—
Federal agency securities	—	—	0.1	0.1	0.1	0.2	—	—	—
State and local government bonds	1.0	0.9	0.6	0.7	0.3	0.2	0.7	1.5	1.1
Corporate bonds	0.1	—	—	—0.1	0.3	0.6	0.6	0.6	1.0
Corporate stocks	0.1	0.3	0.4	0.5	0.3	—0.1	0.1	0.9	0.7*
Total	$1.2	$1.3	$1.2	$1.3	$1.1	$0.9	$1.6	$2.2	$2.8

*Estimated.
Sources: Best Co., Inc., *Best's Aggregates and Averages, Property-Liability*; Bankers Trust Company, *The Investment Outlook* (annual). Stocks are shown net of change in market values. Some columns do not add to totals because of rounding.

Pension and Retirement Plans

DURING the postwar period, pension and retirement plans of all types have become very important investors in the capital markets. In this chapter, we are concerned chiefly with trusteed (noninsured) corporate pension funds and those of state and local governments. A short section on Federal insurance and retirement funds is also included.

All capital-market instruments are found in the growing accumulations of retirement systems. Perhaps the most important development has been the greater interest in common stocks—except in the case of the Federal accounts, which acquire Treasury obligations only.

Trusteed Corporate Pension Funds

Nature and Scope

The importance of pension funds to the economy and to the capital markets is tremendous. Possibly 200,000 plans are now in operation. At the end of 1968, the assets of all public and private pension and retirement funds totaled $214 billions. The most substantial growth since World War II is in private pension and deferred profit-sharing plans. They numbered over 165,000, and their reserves totaled $115 billions (at book value) at the end of 1968.

Private pension plans differ widely in a number of aspects, such as employees covered, service and age requirements for eligibility, retirement provisions, and vesting privileges. Our chief interest, however, lies in the sources and uses of funds and in their impact in the capital markets.

For our purposes plans can be classified as follows: (1) total private pension and profit-sharing plans (including those of companies, unions, and nonprofit organizations) versus corporate pension plans in particular; and (2) insured versus uninsured, or trusteed, corporate plans. The funds of insured corporate plans are invested in annuities and so are comingled with the other assets of life insurance companies.[1] Uninsured plans are usually administered by, or are at least in the custodianship of, bank trustees.

Table 5-1 shows the growth of total private plans since World War II. Their expansion reflects: (1) growth in employment; (2) the increase in the number of persons approaching retirement age and needing protection; (3) the increase in number of plans, indicating acceptance by employers of responsibility for their employees' retirement years; (4) the use of retirement plans—both fixed and profit sharing—as incentives for better work and lower turnover of employees (pension funds became subject to collective bargaining in 1945 through 1950); (5) the need of protection of retirement income from inflation; and (6) the tax

Table 5-1. Selected Data on All Private Retirement Plans, at Year End, 1945–1968,* Billions of Dollars

	1945	1950	1955	1960	1965	1968
Persons covered† (000)	6,400	9,800	15,400	21,200	25,400	28,800‡
Contributions	$1.0	$ 2.1	$ 3.8	$ 5.5	$ 7.8	$ 10.0‡
Benefit payments	0.2	0.4	0.9	1.7	3.2	4.7‡
Reserves (book value):						
Insured plans	2.5	5.6	11.3	18.8	27.3	35.0
Uninsured plans	2.9	6.5	16.1	33.1	58.1	80.3
Total reserves	$5.4	$12.1	$27.4	$51.9	$85.4	$115.3

*Includes multiemployer and union-administered plans and those of nonprofit organizations. Excludes Federal railroad retirement program.
†Excludes those receiving benefits.
‡Estimated.
Sources: U.S. Department of Commerce, *Statistical Abstract of the United States*; Department of Health, Education, and Welfare, Social Security Administration, *Social Security Bulletin;* Securities and Exchange Commission, *Statistical Bulletin.*

[1] Under a ruling by the Securities and Exchange Commission early in 1963, life insurance companies are exempt from its jurisdiction if they restrict annuity arrangements with employers to those involving fixed-income contracts. They may avoid SEC jurisdiction and still segregate the assets representing pension contracts and have their investment free from the usual restrictions on the acquisition of common stocks, providing the risk of market fluctuations is borne by the employer and does not affect the dollar amount of the employees' annuities.

advantages of company plans that meet the eligibility requirements of the Internal Revenue Code, under which contributions are tax exempt to the company and to the employee until retirement.

Persons covered by private plans of all types in early 1969 numbered nearly 29 millions, or 48 per cent of wage and salary workers in private industry, an increase from 32 per cent in 1955 and 42 per cent in 1960. Trusteed plans are more important than insured plans because they offer greater flexibility of investment policy.

Assets of all private noninsured funds, including those of nonprofit organizations, multiemployer funds, and union-administered funds, totaled $80.3 billions (at book value) at the end of 1968. When the reserves of insured plans are added, the aggregate private funds totaled $115 billions.

Sources of Funds: Private Plans

Private plans derive their funds from employer and employee contributions and from net investment earnings. In many cases, all contributions are made by employers and are payments based on wages and salaries or company profits or both. Profit-sharing contributions are found mainly in plans that do not assure the employee a definite stipend upon retirement. As shown in Table 5-1, total contributions to all private plans increased from $1 billion in 1945 to $10 billions (est.) in 1968. From 1960 through 1968, the average annual input was over $7 billions. Most plans are noncontributory by employees. Investment income, exclusive of profit on sale of assets provided an increasing percentage of total receipts (28 per cent in 1968) because capital accumulated faster than did benefit payouts; most workers initially covered by plans are still employed.

Annual Sources of Funds of Noninsured Private Plans

From this point our attention centers on trusteed (noninsured) private plans. These exclude those administered by insurance companies and labor unions but include those of nonprofit organizations and multiemployer plans. Funds available for investment consist of employer and employee contributions and investment income, net of benefits and expenses. The annual data from 1960 through 1968 in Table 5-2 reveal the steady growth of corporate plans, now at around $8 billions per year, or double the 1960 rate. Detailed data on contributions and benefits exclude those for nonprofit and multiemployer plans, whose net receipts are added. Because the coverage of most plans is growing and will continue to do so, for an indefinite period receipts will be well in excess of expenditures. This excess in turn is a dominating factor in investment policy.

In 1968, employers contributed $5.8 billions, or 62 per cent of total

Table 5-2.   Receipts of Private Noninsured Pension Plans,
1960–1968, Billions of Dollars

	1960	1961	1962	1963	1964	1965	1966	1967	1968*
Employer contributions	$3.0	$3.1	$3.2	$3.4	$3.8	$4.4	$4.8	$5.3	$5.8
Employee contributions	0.4	0.4	0.5	0.5	0.5	0.6	0.6	0.7	0.7
Investment and other income	1.2	1.3	1.5	1.6	1.9	2.1	2.4	2.6	2.9
Total receipts	4.6	4.8	5.2	5.5	6.2	7.1	7.8	8.6	9.4
Benefit payments and expenses	1.0	1.2	1.4	1.6	1.8	2.1	2.4	2.7	3.2
Net receipts	$3.6	$3.6	$3.8	$3.9	$4.4	$5.0	$5.4	$5.9	$6.4
Add: Net receipts of nonprofit and multiemployer plans	0.5	0.8	0.6	0.7	1.0	1.1	1.0	1.4	1.6
	$4.1	$4.4	$4.4	$4.6	$5.4	$5.2	$6.4	$7.3	$8.0

*Estimated.
Sources: Social Security Administration, *Social Security Bulletin*; Securities and Exchange Commission, *Statistical Bulletin*; net receipts of nonprofit and multiemployer plans as estimated in Bankers Trust Company, *The Investment Outlook* (annual).

receipts, and employees, $0.7 billions, or 7 per cent for corporate plans alone. Investment income was $2.9 billions, or 31 per cent of receipts, and produced 4 per cent on average market value of assets. Investment income, as we use the term here, excludes realized and unrealized profits or losses on assets. If we include only realized capital gains and relate investment income to book value, the rate of return was 6.0 per cent in 1967.

Deducting from the above sources the annual changes in cash and miscellaneous assets, we have the following sums available for capital-market investment (billions of dollars):

1960	1961	1962	1963	1964	1965	1966	1967	1968
$3.7	$3.7	$3.9	$4.1	$4.4	$5.2	$5.5	$6.0	$6.6 (est.)

Uses of Funds: Investment Policy

The growing accumulation of corporate pension fund capital reflects the increase in the number of plans and number of persons covered and the lag of outgo behind receipts of established plans. Since the middle 1950's, payments to beneficiaries have about equaled investment income alone. Expansion of the assets of trusteed corporate plans in recent years is indicated in Table 5-3. At book value, assets grew $4 billions per year from 1950 through 1968. At market value, they grew $55 billions, or 20 per cent per year, from 1960 through 1968. The rate of growth is second only to that of savings and loan associations. This very large and increasing aggregate of capital makes pension funds a major demand component in the capital markets.

Group figures hide the wide range in investment policy of individual funds. Some hold only Federal bonds; others consist entirely of common stocks. It is apparent that there is a continued swing into common stocks. At the end of 1968, these constituted about 50 per cent of total assets at book value and 62 per cent at market value, compared to 20 per cent (at book) in 1955.

Trusteed funds are in the custodianship of bank trust departments and are invested within the framework of trust regulations. The trust agreement may allow complete freedom. Even in nondiscretionary funds, however, wide latitude is provided by the agreements and by the "prudent-man" rule in effect in the important states. In general, investment policy permits sufficient flexibility to take into account changes in the markets and the business cycle. These factors are especially important to funds emphasizing common stocks; even in these the steady inflow of cash permits the use of dollar cost averaging. Some funds buy stocks every day. Others vary the proportions in cash, fixed-income securities, and equities according to a rough or an exact formula.

Investment policy is also affected by the sources of funds and by whether the benefits are to be fixed or variable. More risk can be taken with company-contributed funds and in plans whose benefits are not determined on an actuarial basis. If inflation hedging is an important goal, a substantial investment in common stocks is appropriate.

Table 5-3. Assets of Uninsured Private Pension Funds,*
1950–1968, Billions of Dollars

	1950 Book	1955 Book	1960 Book	1960 Market	1965 Book	1965 Market	1968 Book	1968 Market
Cash and deposits	$ 0.3	$ 0.5	$ 0.5	$ 0.9	$ 0.9	$ 1.6	$00.0	$ 1.6
U.S. government securities	2.0	3.0	2.7	2.7	3.1	3.0	2.5	2.4
Federal agency securities }	2.8	7.8	0.5	0.4	0.7	0.6	0.7	0.6
Corporate bonds }			15.2	14.2	22.0	20.9	25.5	21.1
Preferred stock	0.3	0.6	0.8	0.7	0.8	0.8	1.3	1.3
Common stock:								
Own company }	0.8	3.3	0.9	2.0	1.7	4.4	2.8	5.7
Other companies }			9.8	13.8	22.7	34.5	37.4	52.2
Mortgages	0.1	0.3	1.3	1.3	3.3	3.3	3.9	3.4
Other assets	0.2	0.6	1.4	1.4	2.8	2.9	4.5	4.3
Total assets	$ 6.5	$16.1	$33.1	$37.1	$58.1	$71.4	$80.5	$92.7

*Includes all corporate funds except those administered by insurance companies; includes plans of nonprofit organizations and multiemployer plans. Some columns do not add to totals because of rounding.

Sources: Social Security Administration, *Social Security Bulletin*; Securties and Exchange Commission, *Statistical Bulletin*.

Cash position   Funds differ greatly in the degree of liquidity maintained. Cash held (including commercial paper) reflects both investment policy and rate of growth. In 1968 and 1969 for funds as a group, the continued weakness in the bond market (reflected in declining bond prices) and continued growth of total assets sent the cash balances to an unusually high proportion of assets.

United States government securities   The proportion of total pension fund assets in Federal securities, at book value, declined from 31 per cent in 1951 to 3 per cent in 1968. This decline reflects recognition of three factors: (1) that growing funds need little liquidity since payouts lag far behind cash receipts and both receipts and benefits are subject to forecasts; (2) that the rate of yield is important—the assets of the fund are expected to grow through compounding of income as well as through new contributions; a difference of 1 per cent in average yield (e.g., an increase from 4 to 5 per cent) can mean as much as 25 per cent in the size of the eventual accumulation; (3) that common stocks may provide both growth and eventual higher income. At the end of 1968, trusteed funds held less than 1 per cent of marketable Federal debt. Impact on the Treasury bond market is negligible.

Corporate bonds   Fixed-income securities such as corporate bonds continue, however, to have an important place in most portfolios. Their steady income, plus cash from spacing of maturities, provides for current expenses and benefits. A solid backlog of such investments is especially important for funds that guarantee the repayment of employees' contributions, for large withdrawals in profit-sharing plans, and for the payment of vested benefits on death, withdrawal, or early retirement of participants.

Although corporate bonds continue to find favor with many pension fund managers, they have declined as a percentage of total assets from 48 per cent at book value in 1955 to 32 per cent at book value and 23 per cent at market value at the end of 1968.

The drastic decline in the prices of bonds in 1966 and subsequent years, reflecting sharply increased yields, has caused a new look at the safety of these securities. In addition, pension fund managers have been caught up in the fetish for "performance" and have turned to growth stocks as a result. Nevertheless, fund holdings of corporate bonds in 1968 constituted (at market value) 14 per cent of corporate bonds outstanding (see Chapter 9). If the high bond yields prevailing in 1969 persist and if the prices of common stocks fail to regain a substantial upward march after the weaknesses in 1969, corporate bonds may attract more attention than has been the case in recent years.

Data on the maturity of corporate bonds held by insured funds are not available. However, it can be assumed that where there is little need for liquidity the emphasis has been on intermediate- and long-term holdings, as in the case of Federal obligations. Some disillusionment with this policy has been felt during the drastic fall in bond prices in recent years. Although not required to liquidate bonds at low prices, the growing fund is increasingly subject to examination and comparison of market price performance.

Common stock   As suggested previously, pension funds have had their greatest impact in the area of common stocks. The annual growth of this category has averaged $2.8 billions at book value (cost) and $4.8 billions at market value from 1955 through 1968, raising the percentage of total assets from 20 per cent at book and 31 per cent at market in 1955 to 50 and 62 per cent, respectively, at the end of 1968. In 1968, $5.7 billions, or 70 per cent of net receipts, went into stocks.[2] To maintain a ratio of 55–60 per cent in common stocks will require continued investment of two-thirds of the net receipts in this medium. Until the present, pension funds have not needed high dividend yields, being content with a 6 to 8 per cent return from dividends plus capital appreciation. As more funds achieve a 55–60 per cent equity position and as stock yields continue to be low, increasing pressure for capital appreciation is felt. Corporate pension funds remain the most important class of institutional investors in common stocks (see Chapter 10). Their influence is felt mainly in the secondary markets. Unlike insurance companies, noninsured pension funds participate in private placements to only a modest degree, although some of the larger funds are recognizing that sound nonmarketable assets are logical investments for the permanent fixed-income component.

The proportion of total common stock outstanding owned by trusteed funds has grown from 0.6 per cent in 1950 to 5.9 per cent at the end of 1968 (see Chapter 10). The funds are a major influence in the market for stock, and their investment policy, characterized by a relatively slow portfolio turnover, has contributed to a thinning of the market for selected issues, to the general high level of stock prices, and to modest stock yields. However, although they have a long-run point of view in their investment policy and are not much concerned with temporary price changes, they are not willing to pay excessive prices for equities.

Not all funds are as heavily invested in common stocks as the group figures would suggest. The character of a fund is often influenced by the number and type of other benefits enjoyed by the employees of the particular company.

Other investments   Preferred stocks continue to be in relative disfavor. The market yields on higher-grade preferreds are as low as those

---

[2]This was the net increase. In 1968, private noninsured pension funds bought $13.1 and sold $7.3 billions of stocks. Securities and Exchange Commission, *Statistical Bulletin* (May 1969), p. 23.

on high-grade bonds because of their appeal to taxed investment institutions, and they lack appreciation possibilities. Their dividends are
not assured, and they have no fixed maturity.

The low yields on tax-free municipal bonds have no appeal for the
qualified fund whose income is exempt under the Internal Revenue
Code.

Types of investments that may have increasing emphasis are real
estate, shares in mutual funds (for the smaller plans), and mortgages.
The latter totaled only $3.9 billions, or nearly 5 per cent of total
trusteed funds (at book value), at the end of 1968. In large funds the
attractive yields on mortgages offset their higher costs of management
and lack of good marketability. Also, servicing can be left with originating mortgage companies. The use of correspondents will likely increase in future years (see Chapter 11).

Annual Uses of Funds

The data in Table 5-4 show the annual net flows of investable funds
into capital-market assets from 1960 through 1968. The trends indicated previously are apparent: the dramatic flow into common stocks,
the substantial variations in flow of funds into corporate bonds, the
decrease in investment in Federal obligations and a modest annual
increase in mortgages. The funds have their greatest influence in the
secondary corporate bond and stock markets. Their impact on the

**Table 5-4. Annual Net Flow of Investable Funds into Capital-Market
Assets, at Year End, 1960–1968, Billions of Dollars**

	1960	1961	1962	1963	1964	1965	1966	1967	1968*
U.S. govern- ment se- curities	$—0.2	$ —	$0.2	$0.1	$—0.1	$—0.1	$—0.5	$—0.4	$0.2
Federal ageny securities	0.1	—	—	—	—	—	—	—	—0.2
Corporate bonds	1.6	1.2	1.2	1.5	1.6	1.5	1.9	1.0	0.7
Preferred stocks	—	—	—	—	0.1	0.1	—	0.2	0.1
Common stocks	1.9	2.2	2.2	2.2	2.2	3.0	3.7	5.0	5.7
Home mortgages	0.1	0.1	0.1	0.1	0.2	0.2	0.2	—	—
Other mortgages	0.2	0.2	0.2	0.2	0.3	0.4	0.3	0.1	0.1
Total	$ 3.7	$ 3.7	$3.9	$4.1	$ 4.4	$ 5.2	$ 5.5	$ 6.0	$6.6

*Estimated.
Sources: Securities and Exchange Commission, *Statistical Bulletin*; Bankers Trust Company,
Investment Outlook. Some columns do not add to totals because of rounding.

former has recently increased. Their role in the stock market is discussed further in Chapter 10.

State and Local Government Retirement Plans

The wide attention to corporate pension funds has obscured the fact that public retirement funds have also grown rapidly in the postwar period. Total assets of the over 2,100 state and local employee retirement systems have increased from $4.7 billions in 1950 to $43.7 billions at the end of fiscal 1968. These resources are to provide retirement income to over 7 million persons. State and municipal pension funds differ in scope of coverage, employee contributions, vesting provisions, actuarial assumptions, and many other factors. We are concerned chiefly with investment policy.

Sources of Funds

Government and employee contributions and investment income provide the funds for these systems. The estimated annual sources of funds for *calendar years* 1960 through 1968 were as shown in Table 5.5.

Although the net receipts have been substantial (in 1968, 62 per cent of total receipts were brought down to net), many plans are relatively mature, and in recent years the rate of asset growth has lagged behind that of corporate pension funds. Nevertheless, the annual supply of funds to the capital markets is very significant. Deducting the funds allocated to cash and miscellaneous assets, the figures are as follows:

1960	1961	1962	1963	1964	1965	1966	1967	1968
$2.1	$2.2	$2.4	$2.4	$2.8	$2.8	$3.5	$3.4	$4.0

Table 5-5. Annual Sources of Funds, State and Local Government Retirement Plans, 1960–1968, Billions of Dollars

	1960	1961	1962	1963	1964	1965	1966	1967	1968
Government contributions	$1.7	$1.9	$2.1	$2.1	$2.3	$2.5	$2.8	$3.0	$3.6
Employee contributions	1.1	1.2	1.3	1.4	1.5	1.7	1.9	2.0	2.3
Investment income	0.6	0.8	0.9	0.9	1.2	1.3	1.5	1.6	1.8
Total receipts	$3.5	$3.9	$4.3	$4.4	$5.0	$5.5	$6.2	$6.6	$7.7
Benefit payments	1.3	1.5	1.8	1.7	1.9	2.1	2.4	2.6	2.9
Net receipts	$2.2	$2.4	$2.5	$2.7	$3.1	$3.4	$3.8	$4.0	$4.8

Sources: Bankers Trust Company, *The Investment Outlook* (annual); U.S. Department of Commerce, Bureau of the Census, *Government Finances, and Finances of Employee-Retirement Systems of State and Local Governments* (annual). Some columns do not add to totals because of rounding.

Uses of Funds: Investment Policy

Detailed data on the composition of assets are available only for recent years (see Table 5-6). After World War II, Federal, state, and local bonds dominated the assets. The percentage of relative investment in both Federal and municipal bonds began to decline sharply around 1950, while that of corporate bonds increased to 53 per cent of assets as of June 30, 1968. The shift reflected a declining need for liquidity and the superior yields available on high-grade corporate bonds. At the end of 1968 the funds owned about 16 per cent of corporate bonds outstanding. Federal bonds of $6.1 billions constituted about 14 per cent of their total assets; this figure represented 2.6 per cent of marketable Treasury obligations outstanding.

These funds still own nearly $2½ billions of tax-free municipal securities, although they do not need the tax advantage and so sacrifice yield. Political pressure apparently requires investment in such securities in a number of jurisdictions, but their influence in the municipals market will likely continue to decrease, except in some local situations.

In about one-third of the states, funds are now permitted to invest in high-grade listed common stocks, reflecting the need for inflation protection and the minor importance of liquidity. But the mortgage category has shown the greatest relative growth. As fund managers be-

Table 5-6.   Assets of State and Local Government Retirement Funds, Amounts and Percentages, Fiscal Years 1950–1968, Billions of Dollars

	1950		1955		1960		1965		1968	
		Per Cent		Per Cent		Per Cent		Per Cent		Per Cent
Cash	$0.1	2.1	$0.1	1.0	$ 0.2	1.1	$ 0.3	1.0	$ 0.5	1.1
U.S. government bonds	2.6	55.3	4.5	45.0	5.9	32.1	7.4	23.2	6.1	14.0
State and local government bonds	1.5	31.9	2.6	26.0	4.3	23.4	2.7	8.5	2.4	5.5
Corporate bonds					6.1	33.1	15.1	47.5	23.3	53.4
Corporate stocks					0.4	2.2	1.4	4.4	3.3	7.5
	0.5	10.7	2.7	27.0						
Mortgages					1.2	6.5	3.4	10.7	5.3	12.1
Other assets					0.3	1.6	1.5	4.7	2.8	6.4
Total	$4.7	100	$9.9	100	$18.4	100	$31.8	100	$43.7	100

Sources: 1950 data estimated by V. Andrews, "Noninsured Corporate and State and Local Government Retirement Funds in the Financial Structure," in *Private Capital Markets* (Englewood Cliffs, N.J.: Prentice-Hall, Inc., 1964); 1955–1968 data from U.S. Department of Commerce, Bureau of the Census, *Governmental Finances* (annual), and *Finances of Employee-Retirement Systems of State and Local Governments*.

come more familiar with this investment, as legal barriers are removed, and as the funds make greater use of the services of mortgage correspondents, mortgages are likely to be even more attractive.

Annual Uses of Funds

The data in Table 5-7 show the net annual additions to capital-market assets from 1960 through 1968. The data show the vacillating investment in Federal bonds, the steady accumulation of corporate bonds and mortgages, and the decline in holdings of municipal bonds.

The rate of growth of state and local government retirement funds has been exceeded only by that of corporate pension funds and that of savings and loan associations. Although there are some signs of maturity, as government employment, salaries, and benefits continue to increase, these funds will likewise grow. Their increasing interest in high-grade corporate bonds has already made them the most important buyer of publicly marketed securities of this type, especially in very recent years. Their influence in the mortgage market will likely continue to increase as the high yields remain attractive.

Federal Insurance and Retirement Funds

Certain activities of the Federal Treasury qualify it as a financial institution involved in the capital market. It collects receipts and dis-

Table 5-7. Annual Changes in Capital-Market Assets, State and Local Government Retirement Plans, 1960–1968, Billions of Dollars

	1960	1961	1962	1963	1964	1965	1966	1967	1968*
U.S. government securities	$0.4	$ —	$0.3	$0.3	$0.5	$0.1	$—0.3	$—0.4	$—0.5
Federal agency securities	—	0.1	0.1	0.1	—	—	—	—	0.1
State and local government bonds	0.2	0.1	—0.4	—0.4	—0.5	—0.3	—0.1	—0.1	—0.1
Corporate bonds	1.1	1.3	2.0	1.9	2.1	2.0	2.5	2.6	3.1
Corporate stocks	0.1	0.1	0.2	0.2	0.3	0.3	0.5	0.6	0.9
Mortgages	0.3	0.5	0.2	0.4	0.4	0.7	0.8	0.6	0.4
Total	$2.1	$2.2	$2.4	$2.4	$2.8	$2.8	$ 3.5	$ 3.4	$4.0

*Estimated.
  Sources: As converted to calendar year from data in Bankers Trust Company, *The Investment Outlook* (annual), and U.S. Department of Commerce, Bureau of the Census sources. Some columns do not add to totals because of rounding.

penses payments from a variety of funds that support Federal insurance and pension plans. The most important of these funds are the Old-Age and Survivors Insurance Trust Fund, Unemployment Trust Fund, National Service Life Insurance Fund, Civil Service Retirement and Disability Fund, Disability Insurance Trust Fund, and Railroad Retirement Fund.[3] Income of the trust accounts is derived from taxes, premiums, contributions, and interest. Net receipts after benefit payments and expenses are invested mainly in Federal bonds. The big accumulations took place during World War II and the succeeding decade.

Uses of Funds

At the end of selected years, Federal insurance and retirement trust funds owned Federal securities in the amounts shown in Table 5-8.

Table 5-8.   Ownership of Government Securities, Federal Trust Funds, 1950–1968, Billions of Dollars

	1950	1955	1960	1965	1968
Marketable securities	$ 3.7	$ 5.1	$ 5.5	$ 8.1	$10.8
Special issues	32.7	43.1	43.5	45.0	57.1
Total	$36.4	$48.2	$49.0	$53.1	$67.9

Source: *Treasury Bulletin.*

At the end of 1968, the funds held 19 per cent of total direct and guaranteed Federal debt outstanding. Their impact on the Federal Securities market has, however, been minimized because the bulk of their funds is invested in special nonmarketable issues (see Chapter 7).

In recent years the fund assets have grown at a varying rate.[4] The annual net acquisitions of Federal obligations from 1960 to 1968 were as follows (billions of dollars):[5]

1960	1961	1962	1963	1964	1965	1966	1967	1968
$1.2	$—0.6	$0.3	$1.5	$1.6	$1.4	$6.4	$6.0	$2.4

In order to avoid intragovernmental transactions, these changes in trust fund holdings are excluded from the data on annual changes in the ownership of Federal debt on p. 100 and from the master schedule of

---

[3]The Treasury manages a number of other Federal investment accounts and funds of other departments and organizations. Those discussed here are engaged in providing insurance and retirement benefits.

[4]The large increases in 1966 and 1967 reflect increased taxes and contributions resulting from changes in the law such as increased withholdings for Social Security.

[5]Source: *Treasury Bulletin.*

sources and uses of funds in Chapter 12. The Federal funds are not treated as an "institution" in this respect.

It is also important to distinguish the operations of these trust funds from Treasury management of a variety of Federal agencies and sponsored organizations. The role of these agencies in supplying and using capital-market funds is discussed in Chapter 7, and their operations are included in the master data in Chapter 12.

```
666666666666666666666666666666666666666666666666666666666666666666666666666666666666
666666666666666666666666666666666666666666666666666666666666666666666666666666666666
6666666666666666666666666666666    6666666666666    666    6666666666666666666666666666
6666666666666666666666666666666    66666666666    6666    6666666666666666666666666666
6666666666666666666666666666666    666666666    66666    6666666666666666666666666666
6666666666666666666666666666666    6666666    666666    6666666666666666666666666666
6666666666666666666666666666666    66666    6666666    6666666666666666666666666666
6666666666666666666666666666666    666    66666666    6666666666666666666666666666
6666666666666666666666666666666    6    666666666    6666666666666666666666666666
6666666666666666666666666666666        6666666666    6666666666666666666666666666
6666666666666666666666666666666        66666666666    6666666666666666666666666666
666666666666666666666666666666666666666666666666666666666666666666666666666666666666
666666666666666666666666666666666666666666666666666666666666666666666666666666666666
```

Investment Companies

THE great growth of investment companies has been an outstanding
feature of the postwar period. Serving as media through which individual investors acquire a stake in bonds and stocks, they have had a
great influence on investor habits and on the securities markets. Their
role has been to funnel savings into outstanding securities in the secondary markets rather than to finance new capital investment.

General Nature and Types

The investment company pools the funds of investors, obtained
through the sale of shares (and in some cases bonds) in a portfolio of
securities. The portfolio is managed to obtain for the shareholders the
benefits of diversification, professional selection and supervision of
securities, and skilled timing of purchases and sales. The shareholder
hopes, with a small outlay (per share), to attain results superior to those
he could obtain through direct investment.

For these companies, investment is the primary function. Funds are
obtained and managed for this purpose, in contrast to other financial
institutions (such as banks and insurance companies), which invest in
order to meet their obligations, and to holding companies, which acquire stocks for purposes of control.

Investment companies differ widely in size, objectives (such as income versus appreciation), methods of operation, composition of port-

folios (securities held and range of diversification), degree of risk under-
taken, and relations with investors. A classification of main types from
the standpoint of organization and financing is as follows:

(1) Fixed. Here (using the trust form of organization) shares represent ownership of a portfolio over which management has little or no
discretion.

(2) Management. This group, to which our discussion will be confined, involves companies whose managements, within the limits of announced policy and legal regulation, adjust the portfolio to obtain
superior results for shareholders. There are two major categories:

(a) Open-end, or "mutual" funds. Such organizations make a continuous offering of new shares at prices to net the issuer their net asset
value. The share capitalization is "open." Shares are redeemable at net
asset value on very short notice. Such companies do not issue bonds or
preferred stock. The investor in the shares of mutual funds acquires
them from the company or from distributing dealers. There is no open-
market trading. The market for their sale is the issuing company,
through the privilege of redemption.

(b) Closed-end. Such companies have a fixed capitalization. Funds
are obtained originally from the sale of common stock and, in the case
of "leverage" companies, bonds or preferred stock or both and bank
loans. Shares are traded on the listed and over-the-counter markets.

The statements of open-end (mutual) and of most closed-end companies show their securities portfolio at market value. Asset growth of
an individual mutual fund thus represents (a) excess of shares issued,
sold to existing and new shareholders, over shares redeemed; and (b)
any increase in the market value of the portfolio. The open-end company must engage in constant sales activity to prevent redemptions from
shrinking the asset value of the fund. Dollar growth of a closed-end
company reflects occasional new financing and the rising market value
of portfolio assets.

(3) A minor type of company sells face-amount certificates, which
are designed to reach a set dollar amount at the maturity of the contract.

The degree of diversification, types of securities held, amount of risk
assumed, and investment purposes of the company are interrelated and
are all reflected in its securities portfolio. Closed-end companies are
classifiable into two major types: (a) diversified, with portfolio consisting of a broad array of securities, mainly common stocks; and (b) those
whose portfolios consist mostly of special situation investments. Mutual
companies present the greatest variety of investments. One classification
of such companies, by general portfolio distribution, at the end of 1968
is shown in Table 6-1.[1]

---

[1]For a more detailed earlier breakdown of types of funds by number and assets,
1952 through 1958, see *A Study of Mutual Funds*, prepared for the Securities and
Exchange Commission by the Wharton School of Finance and Commerce. 87th
Cong., 2d sess. (Washington, D.C.: Government Printing Office, 1962), p. 116.

Growth and Size

The number of all investment companies had grown from 366 at the end of 1945 to over 800 at the end of 1968, and total assets had increased from $3 billions to $62 billions. The big expansion was in the mutual, or open-end, company, with net assets of $57 billions. Net assets of the 240 members of the Investment Company Institute rose from $1.3 billions in 1945 to $52.7 billions at the end of 1968; the number of shareholders' accounts (including duplications) exceeded 9 millions, representing over 4 million individual and institutional investors.

This postwar expansion reflects a number of factors: the general economic progress of the period, the growth in total savings, the rise in stock market values, the aggressive sales promotion of mutual fund shares, and their appeal for a variety of reasons including the desire (through common stocks) to offset inflation. Other factors include the increase in the number and types of funds and the appeal of a growing number of conveniences and services such as accumulation plans and dividend reinvestment arrangements. The general acceptance by the public has also been a function of operating results and of the growth of public interest in securities investments in general.

Basic Sources of Funds

Closed-end companies, as a group, grow relatively slowly because of their fixed capitalizations. Occasionally new securities are sold. A number of those with bonds and preferred stock outstanding have retired all or part of such senior securities and so have been partially liquidating.[2] Some have also repurchased common shares. The major factor of dollar

Table 6-1. Composition of Open-End (Mutual) Funds, 1968, Billions of Dollars

Type	Number	Net Assets	Per Cent
Common stock:			
Maximum capital gain	120	$ 7.9	14.0
Growth	100	15.5	27.2
Growth and income	81	20.2	35.5
Specialized	27	1.6	2.7
Balanced	31	7.7	13.6
Income	27	2.1	3.7
Tax-free exchange	30	1.6	2.8
Bond and preferred	8	0.3	0.5
	424	$56.9	100

Source: Arthur Wiesenberger & Co., *Investment Companies* (New York, 1969), p. 44. International funds are excluded.

growth has been the general rise in market value of stock holdings. Net assets of closed-end companies totaled $5.2 billions at the end of 1968, an increase from less than $1 billion at the end of 1945. About half of this growth represented increased market value rather than expansion. A new type of closed-end company appeared in 1967—the so-called capital-leveraged, or "duo," fund. Two types of shares were issued, contributing equal amounts to initial capital: capital shares, which receive all capital appreciation, and income shares, which receive all net investment income and have a cumulative dividend requirement and a redemption date.

Mutual funds expand by selling more shares than they redeem. In each postwar year, for open-end companies as a group (but not for all individual companies), sales of shares exceeded repurchases. See Table 6-2 for the data on the net sales (gross sales less redemption) for 5-year periods and for recent years since 1950 that show how much variation in year-end asset values can be attributed to growth through sales and how much to change in market value of portfolio assets ($ millions). Net assets are total assets less all liabilities—that is, the liquidating value of portfolios, at market.

From 1950 through 1968, the market value of open-end companies increased $50.2 billions, from $2.5 (1950) to $52.7 billions. Of this increase, $20 billions are attributable to net sales of new shares.[3] The years 1954 through 1958 were characterized by nationwide fluctuations

Table 6-2.   Net Assets and Net Sales, Mutual Investment Companies, 1950–1968, Millions of Dollars

	Total Change in Net Assets	Excess of Sales Over Redemptions	Asset Change Attributable to Market
1950–1954	+$4,116	$2,074	+$2,042
1955–1959	+ 9,709	5,266	+ 4,443
1960	+ 1,208	1,255	− 47
1961	+ 5,763	1,791	+ 3,972
1962	− 1,518	1,576	− 3,094
1963	+ 3,943	954	+ 2,989
1964	+ 3,902	1,529	+ 2,373
1965	+ 6,104	2,396	+ 3,708
1966	− 391	2,666	− 3,057
1967	+ 9,872	1,926	+ 7,946
1968	+ 7,976	2,981	+ 4,995

Sources: Derived from data in Arthur Wiesenberger & Co., *Investment Companies* (annual), and Investment Company Institute, *Mutual Fund Fact Book* (annual).

[2]In 8 of the 10 years 1945–1954, inclusive, repurchases exceeded new capital. Net capital (including bank loans) increased only $138 millions. But in each year from 1955 to 1967, there was a net capital increase. The total for the period was $537 millions. Investment Company Institute, *Investment Companies: A Statistical Summary, 1940–1960* (New York, 1961); *Moody's Bank and Finance Manual* (1969), p. a55.
[3]Data are for members of the Investment Company Institute.

in the market value of investment company assets, but the rate of in-flow from the sale of new shares still showed stability (13 to 16 per cent of asset totals).[4] From 1961 through 1968, the market was the chief influence on asset values. But even in years of sharp market decline like 1962 and 1966, industry sales exceeded redemptions. The experience of individual companies, of course, varied.

Annual Sources of Funds

The annual net growth in the assets of mutual funds, derived from the excess of sales of capital shares over redemptions (investment income is all distributed in dividends), for 1960 through 1968, was as shown in Table 6-3.

The declining trend in sales of new shares that began in 1962, accompanied by a higher rate of redemptions, produced a substantial drop in net sales. The decrease in 1962 is attributable mainly to the break in stock market prices. Its continuation in 1963 reflected the shift of investor interest to individual securities, their general apathy toward new commitments in stocks (see Chapter 10), and public reaction to the critical Wharton Study. Net sales recovered to $1.5 billions in 1964 and increased until 1967, when the 1966–1967 weakness in the stock market, together with shareholders' need for funds, sharply reduced net sales. But they rebounded to all-time heights in 1968. If we deduct the changes in cash and other assets (net of liabilities), sources for capital-market assets were (billions of dollars) the following:

1960	1961	1962	1963	1964	1965	1966	1967	1968
$1.2	$1.4	$1.5	$0.8	$1.1	$1.6	$2.0	$1.1	$2.4

Uses of Funds

Investment companies operate almost solely in the capital markets. With the exception of short-term bank borrowings of a few closed-end companies, new funds are raised from long-term sources (sale of securi-

Table 6-3.   Net Sales of Mutual Funds, 1960–1968, Billions of Dollars

	1960	1961	1962	1963	1964	1965	1966	1967	1968
Sale of shares	$2.1	$3.0	$2.7	$2.5	$3.4	$4.4	$4.7	$4.6	$6.8
Redemptions	0.8	1.2	1.1	1.5	1.9	2.0	2.0	2.7	3.8
Net Sales	$1.3	$1.8	$1.6	$1.0	$1.5	$2.4	$2.7	$1.9	$3.0

Sources: Investment Company Institute, *Mutual Fund Fact Book;* Arthur Wiesenberger & Co., *Investment Companies.*

[4]Wharton School of Finance and Commerce, *A Study of Mutual Funds,* p. 4.

ties) and are invested mainly in the secondary securities markets, that is, in outstanding rather than in new issues. In contrast to other institutional groups—for example, savings and loan associations, whose members are much alike—investment companies differ very widely in objectives and portfolio composition. No generalizations as to the character of their assets are feasible, except to say that as a group the bulk of their money is placed in common stocks. Funds that buy only common stocks or that are predominantly stock funds are in the majority; they are also the very large funds and so dominate the group data. Investment in common stocks ran about $44 billions at the end of 1968.

Mutual funds are the major factor in the secondary securities markets. The emphasis for the group continues to be placed on common stocks, with some slight increase in the proportion of common stocks to total assets in recent years. This proportion is, of course, affected by changes in market value.

The combined balance sheets of mutual funds (ICI members) and their relative proportions at selected year ends are shown in Table 6-4. (Cash is shown net of all liabilities.) The burgeoning dollar growth of these funds shows up almost entirely in common stocks; their proportion of total net assets reached 84 per cent at the end of 1968. One should, of course, remember that the group figures are not typical of all individual funds, which differ greatly in portfolio composition, and that funds specializing in common stocks dominate the combined data.

Annual Portfolio Changes

The data in Table 6-5 show the annual net accumulation of capital-market securities by mutual funds from 1960 through 1968. Government bond acquisitions have varied through the years, reflecting the need of the mutual funds for liquidity and their policy with respect

Table 6-4. Combined Net Assets of Open-End Investment Companies,* Amounts and Percentages, at Year End, 1950–1968, Billions of Dollars

	1950		1955		1960		1965		1968	
		Per Cent		Per Cent		Per Cent		Per Cent		Per Cent
Net cash	$0.1	4.2	$0.2	2.6	$ 0.4	2.4	$ 1.0	2.8	$ 2.1	4.0
U.S. government securities	0.1	4.1	0.2	2.5	0.6	3.5	0.8	2.3	1.1	2.1
Corporate bonds ⎫			0.5	6.4	1.2	7.0	2.5	7.3	3.4	6.5
Preferred stocks ⎬	2.2	91.7	0.5	6.4	0.7	4.1	0.6	1.7	1.7	3.2
Common stocks ⎭			6.4	82.1	14.1	83.0	30.3	85.9	44.4	84.2
Total	$2.4	100	$7.8	100	$17.0	100	$35.2	100	$52.7	100

*1950 data, all open-end companies; 1955 through 1968 data, Investment Company Institute (ICI) members only. Data exclude exchange funds and international funds.

Sources: Securities and Exchange Commission, *Statistical Bulletin* (1950 data); Investment Company Institute; Arthur Wiesenberger & Co., *Investment Companies* (annual).

Table 6-5.   Annual Changes in Capital-Market Assets, Mutual Funds,
              1960–1968, Billions of Dollars

	1960	1961	1962	1963	1964	1965	1966	1967	1968
U.S. government securities	$0.1	$ —	$0.3	$ —	$ —	$ —	$ 0.6	$—0.4	$ 0.6
Corporate bonds	0.2	0.3	0.2	0.1	0.3	0.4	0.4	0.1	0.6
Preferred stocks	—	0.1	—	—	—	—0.1	—0.1	—	—0.1
Common stocks	0.8	1.0	1.0	0.7	0.8	1.3	1.1	1.4	1.3
Total	$1.2	$1.4	$1.5	$0.8	$1.1	$ 1.6	$ 2.0	$ 1.1	$ 2.4

Sources: Investment Company Institute; Arthur Wiesenberger & Co., *Investment Companies* (annual); Bankers Trust Company, *The Investment Outlook* (annual). Data do not reflect changes in market value. Some columns do not add to totals because of rounding.

to full investment. In years like 1964 and 1966, when the stock market was very weak, government and corporate bonds soaked up much of the continuing inflow of new funds. In 1968 and 1969 bonds were attractive for high yields, while net acquisition of common stocks suffered from the uncertainty of market conditions. Preferred stocks have continued to lose favor, being unattractive for income and (except for convertibles) lacking the appreciation possibilities of common stock. In 1969 the general decline in stock prices caused many funds to increase their cash positions in expectation of later buying opportunities.

Influence in the Capital Market

The impact of investment companies is primarily in the secondary market for corporate stocks. At the end of 1968, listed holdings of mutual and closed-end companies combined represented 6 per cent of the value of all stocks listed on the New York Stock Exchange. Mutual funds alone held $37 billions, or 5.3 per cent of the list.[5]

The contribution of mutual funds to stock trading activity has accelerated greatly in recent years. Purchase transactions have exceeded sales in each year since 1955, and net acquisitions totaled $1.6 billions in 1968. In 1968, the average of purchases and sales totaled $19.7 billions, an increase of 37 per cent over 1967. This average equaled 13.6 per cent of the total stock volume on the New York Stock Exchange.[6]

The activity rate of stock market trading by the mutual funds was the highest rate for all institutional investors in 1968—46 per cent for the year and 56 per cent on an annual basis in the fourth quarter. These percentages mean that the funds traded half of their portfolio holdings during the year.[7] The rate declined somewhat in 1969.

[5]New York Stock Exchange, *Fact Book, 1969,* p. 45. The Securities and Exchange Commission estimates that at the end of 1968, investment companies owned 8 per cent of all common stock outstanding. Securities and Exchange Commission, *Statistical Bulletin* (May 1969), p. 26.

[6]New York Stock Exchange, *Fact Book, 1969,* pp. 5, 46.

As for the influence of investment companies on stock prices, the Investment Company Institute claims that they have contributed stability. This source reports that in all but 2 of the 13 periods of stock market decline during 1945–1966, investors purchased more mutual fund shares than they sold (thus contributing net capital for investment in common stocks), and the companies themselves, on balance, increased rather than decreased their portfolios.[8] From a much more detailed study of trading activities, the Wharton report concludes that "it is not possible to characterize the trading behavior of mutual funds in response to prior or concurrent fluctuations in stock prices as preponderantly stabilizing or destabilizing, although there is some evidence of a destabilizing influence in price decline prior to the lows."[9]

Further discussion of the impact of investment companies in the common stock market is found in Chapter 10.

Securities and Exchange Commission, *Statistical Bulletin* (May 1969), pp. 21–22. The activity rate is the average of purchases and sales divided by the average market value of stockholdings at the beginning and end of the year.

[8]Investment Company Institute, *Mutual Fund Fact Book, 1969*, pp. 36–37.

[9]Wharton School of Commerce and Finance, *A Study of Mutual Funds*, p. 23.

The Federal Securities Market

Our discussion of the Federal securities market emphasizes the obligations of the United States Treasury. Because they are closely related, the ungaranteed securities of Federal agencies are also considered. These agencies could be classed as financial institutions along with those that were discussed previously. For simplicity, their role as suppliers as well as users of long-term funds is combined in one section at the end of this chapter.

United States Obligations

The whole subject of Federal financing and debt management and its interrelations with monetary policy is very complex. This discussion can include only a summary of Federal borrowing policy, along with the demand, ownership, and yield aspects of the Federal securities market.

Much of Federal debt is intermediate or long term in maturity. But it is difficult arbitrarily to consider this portion separately from the short term. Maturities of all lengths are held by institutions for income and liquidity. Our discussion, however, emphasizes the capital market, or long-term, aspects of this important Federal market.

Types and Trends of Total Federal Debt

The direct and guaranteed debt of the Federal government at the end of selected years is shown in Table 7-1. Treasury bills are issued on a discount basis and are sold for cash at auction through the Federal Reserve banks. Their maturity ranges from 3 months to 1 year. One-year bills were first issued in 1959. Certificates of indebtedness bear one coupon paying interest and principal at maturity, which is usually 1 year. Their volume has been small since the issuance of 1-year Treasury bills began. Treasury notes are coupon instruments with maturities of from 1 to 5 years. They are issued for cash and for refinancing. Treasury bonds have original maturities of over 5 years. Only the fully market-able issues are eligible for purchase by all investors. They are often callable 5 years before maturity. The remaining Federal obligations are nonmarketable (nonnegotiable) and so their supply has only an indirect effect on market yields. Savings bonds currently being issued are Series E (discount bonds) and Series H (interest paid by check). Both of these bonds yielded (mid-1969) 4.25 per cent to full maturity (7 years). (In July 1969, the Treasury asked Congress to raise the yield to a more competitive 5 per cent by reducing the maturity to 5 years, 10 months.) Treasury bond "investment series" are sold to large institu-

Table 7-1. Public Debt and Guaranteed Obligations of the United States Government, at Year End, 1950–1968, Billions of Dollars

	1950	1955	1960	1965	1968
Marketable:					
Bills	$ 13.6	$ 22.3	$ 39.5	$ 60.2	$ 75.0
Certificates	5.4	15.7	18.4	—	—
Notes	39.3	43.3	51.3	50.2	76.5
Bonds	94.2	81.9	79.8	104.2	85.3
Total	$152.5	$163.2	$189.0	$214.6	$236.8
Nonmarketable:					
Savings bonds	$ 58.0	$ 57.9	$ 47.2	$ 50.3	$ 52.3
Treasury bonds (savings and investment series)*	9.6	12.3	6.2	2.8	2.5
Special issues	33.7	43.9	44.3	46.3	59.1
Miscellaneous	0.5	0.4	0.1	2.5	1.9
Total	$101.8	$114.5	$ 97.8	$101.9	$115.8
Matured and noninterest-bearing debt	2.4	3.0	3.4	4.4	5.4
Guaranteed debt	—	0.1	0.2	0.5	0.6
Total direct and guaranteed debt	$256.7	$280.8	$290.4	$321.4	$358.6

*Special series Treasury bonds in 1950 were composed mostly of Treasury tax and savings series notes.
Source: *Treasury Bulletin.*

tional investors and are convertible into marketable Treasury notes. Special issues are sold directly to various government trust funds. Guaranteed debt now consists solely of bonds of the Federal Housing Administration.

Growth of the Federal Debt

The Federal debt rose from $43 billions in June 1940 to its wartime peak of $278 billions in fiscal 1945–1946. This enormous expansion was the result of wartime deficit financing. Peace brought a temporary decline in debt to $253 billions at the end of 1948, followed by increases in all but 4 years through 1963. In the 23-year period from 1946 through 1968, only 6 years (1947, 1948, 1951, 1956, 1957, and 1960) showed budget surpluses. During this period, however, the debt increased by only $80 billions. Of this increase, $49 billions came in 1963 through 1968 as the result of expanded domestic programs and the war in Viet Nam.

At the end of 1968, the marketable categories constituted $236.8 billions of the total debt of $358.6 billions. After deducting the $18.1 billions of marketable debt held by Federal agencies and trust funds (in addition to their holdings of special issues), the debt involved in the money and capital markets, including holdings by the Federal Reserve banks, totaled $218.7 billions; $108.6 billions had a maturity of less than 1 year, so that the "capital-market" debt was $110.1 billions.

Reference to Table 1-2 shows that in the postwar period the Federal debt has not increased at the same rate as have other long-term instruments. This lack of growth has facilitated the direction of institutional investment funds into the municipal and private capital markets.

Shifts in Types and Maturities

The variations in total Federal debt have not been accompanied by similar changes in marketable debt or its various maturity classes. The data in Table 7-2 show the composition of public marketable debt at selected year ends. From 1945 through 1950, marketable debt declined much more than did total debt. Much of it was retired from excess cash balances and refinanced by the issuance of Savings and Investment Series bonds. In part, the shift offset the emphasis of the Treasury on short maturities stemming from the pegging of the yields on long-term bonds so that a large supply overhung the market. Early in 1951, large-scale exchange of 2.5 per cent marketable Treasury bonds for Investment Series bonds supported the "accord" with the Federal Reserve, which released the marketable debt from maximum yields. Nonmarketable debt reached a postwar high of $115 billions, or 45 per cent of the total debt, as of June 1951, while marketable debt reached its postwar low of $138 billions, or 55 per cent of the total. Nonmarketable debt,

Table 7-2.   Composition of Federal Marketable Debt,
1950–1968, Billions of Dollars

	1950	1955	1960	1965	1968
Within a year	$ 58.0	$ 60.6	$ 73.8	$ 93.4	$108.6
1–5 years	33.4	38.3	72.3	60.6	68.3
5–10 years	17.4	31.4	18.7	35.0	35.1
10–20 years	43.7	32.9	13.2	8.5	8.4
Over 20 years	—	—	11.0	17.1	16.4
Total marketable	$152.5	$163.2	$189.0	$214.6	$236.8
Less—held by Federal agencies and trust funds	5.4	4.2	8.1	13.4	18.1
"Public marketable"	$147.1	$159.0	$180.9	$201.2	$218.7

Sources: *Treasury Bulletin; Federal Reserve Bulletin.* Data for 1950 are classified by first call date; for 1955 through 1968, by final maturity. It should be noted that these data show the maturity classifications outstanding, not those at time of issue. A bond issued over 19 years ago with a maturity of 20 years would be included in the within a year category.

especially savings bonds and special issues, continued to increase into 1954 but declined in relative importance.

Between 1955 and 1968, a very substantial shift took place in marketable obligations. All major categories of nonmarketable securities, except special issues, declined, but the main shrinkage was in Savings bonds, which showed regular net reductions, and in Treasury bonds, Investment Series, which were gradually converted or retired. At the end of 1968, the proportion of major categories of total debt were as follows: marketable, 66 per cent; nonmarketable, 32 per cent (including savings bonds, 15 per cent, and special issues, 17 per cent); matured and guaranteed, 2 per cent.

The shifting internal composition of the debt has an important impact on yields. A planned increase in the supply of marketable types, resulting in increased yields, is not offset by demand for Savings bonds whose yields have become increasingly unattractive. Funds are more likely to move into other savings media or into capital-market securities, and the holdings of special issues in government trust funds are in effect inpounded. Yields on government bonds, therefore, reflect changes in marketable debt outstanding rather than in total debt.

The data in Tables 7-1 and 7-2 reveal the increasing importance of debt with maturity of 5 years or less. Marketable treasury bonds, whose original maturity is over 5 years, have not been issued in recent years because of the statutory limit on their coupons of 4¼ per cent. Market yields have been higher than this since 1965.

As a result of Treasury policy to finance with shorter maturities, debt due within a year increased from 38 to 46 per cent of marketable debt from 1950 through 1968. Intermediate debt of 1 to 5 years maturity increased almost twofold during 1955–1960, but declined to 29 per cent in 1968, while 5-to-10-year debt fell to 15 per cent in June 1969. Debt due in 10 years or more constituted only 9 per cent of the total, compared with 28 per cent in 1950. Short maturities have been emphasized during periods of economic expansion, when the passage of time also moved intermediate maturities forward. Medium maturities have been emphasized during periods of monetary ease such as 1953 through 1955, 1957 through 1958, and 1967.

Space does not permit an account of all the shifts in the various maturity classes in the postwar period. Movements in Treasury financing to add to or to detract from the supply of different classes have reflected an attempt to balance the debt structure to minimize the total interest bill. The cyclical debt management policy of the Treasury with respect to maturities, although exerting now an upward and now a downward pressure on long-term yields, has in general followed the climate of the market.

Organization of the Primary Market

The Federal Reserve banks serve as agents of the Treasury in issuing (and redeeming) government securities. Each new issue is announced by press statements of the Secretary of the Treasury, and the Federal Reserve banks send out descriptive circulars to commercial banks, dealers, and other possible buyers. Only about 17 important dealers have major activity in the government securities market—5 commercial banks and 12 nonbank securities firms.

New issues of Treasury bills are offered at auction weekly through the Federal Reserve banks and their branches. The Secretary of the Treasury invites tenders for purchase on a discount basis below par and accepts bids from the highest price down until the approximate amount of funds stated in the offering circular is obtained. Federal Reserve banks themselves may make bids to the limit of the maturing bills they hold.

Other marketable issues are sold at par at a specified rate of interest determined after analysis of the market and consultation with banks and other institutions. The government enters the market in competition with other users of capital and must pay the required yield, although this yield is influenced by Treasury debt management and Federal Reserve open-market policy. The Federal Reserve banks receive the applications of dealers, banks, and others, and make allotments in accordance with instructions from the Treasury. They also receive payment for the securities and deposit the proceeds to Treasury accounts.

Volume and Buyers of New Federal Government Securities

Each year the Federal Treasury undertakes sufficient financing to cover deficits and refunding and to keep its cash balance satisfactory. In most years, the total volume of financing substantially exceeds that of the combined state and local governments, and in some years, that of corporations. The net increases (or decreases) in outstanding debt (after refunding) do not correspond with Treasury budget surpluses and deficits because these in turn do not correspond with changes in Treasury cash balances. The balances reflect public and intragovernmental cash transactions, including transactions with government trust funds.

The data in Table 7-3 show the gross proceeds of new issues adjusted for refinancing and redemption (which in some years resulted in debt reduction) and for intragovernmental transfers and changes in Treasury cash balances. By deducting changes in government trust fund holdings (mostly special issues), the net annual changes in publicly held securities, including, for this purpose, those held by Federal agencies, are derived. In years like 1961, 1962, 1964, and 1966 through 1969, the substantial growth of the Federal debt, in competition with the needs of state and local governments, business, and individuals (for mortgages), contributed to the increased interest rates that characterized those periods (see pp. 156–57).

The discussion of the composition and the changes in the ownership of Federal obligations in the previous chapters did not reveal the holdings of various maturities by all categories of investors. Even if the data were available, a discussion of the shift of funds between short- and long-term Federal obligations in all institutions would present too many complexities for this short book. The data in Table 7-4 on annual net acquisitions of government securities (excluding those of Treasury

Table 7-3. Annual Changes in Publicly Held U.S. Government Securities, 1960–1968, Billions of Dollars

	1960	1961	1962	1963	1964	1965	1966	1967	1968
Gross proceeds, new issues	$7.9	$12.3	$8.6	$10.8	$10.7	$9.3	$8.2	$19.4	$17.6
Less—refinancing, intragovernmental financing and changes in cash	8.5	6.2	1.1	4.7	2.1	6.6	−0.2	4.0	4.2
Change in gross debt	−0.6	6.1	7.5	6.1	8.6	2.7	8.4	15.4	13.4
Less—change in U.S. government trust accounts	1.2	−0.6	0.7	1.5	1.6	1.4	6.4	6.0	2.4
Change in U.S. government securities not in Treasury trusts	$−1.8	$6.7	$8.2	$4.6	$7.0	$1.3	$2.0	$9.4	$11.0

Sources: *Federal Reserve Bulletin; Treasury Bulletin.*

Table 7-4.   Annual Acquisitions of U.S. Government Securities, 1960–1968, Billions of Dollars

	1960	1961	1962	1963	1964	1965	1966	1967	1968
Commercial banks	$2.1	$5.6	$—0.2	$—3.1	$—0.3	$—3.4	$—3.4	$6.4	$2.2
Federal Reserve banks	0.7	1.5	1.9	2.8	3.4	3.8	3.5	4.8	3.8
Mutual savings banks	—0.6	—0.1	—	—0.2	—0.1	—0.3	—0.7	—0.4	—0.5
Savings and loan associations	0.1	0.6	0.4	0.9	0.5	0.5	0.4	1.5	0.3
Life insurance companies	—0.4	—0.3	—	—0.4	—0.2	—0.5	—0.3	—0.2	—0.2
Property and liability insurance companies	—	—	0.1	—	0.1	—	0.2	—0.8	—
Corporate pension funds	—0.2	—	0.2	0.1	—0.1	—0.1	—0.5	—0.4	0.2
State and local retirement funds	0.4	—	0.3	0.3	0.5	0.1	—0.3	—0.4	—0.5
Investment companies	0.1	—	0.3	—	—	—	0.6	—0.4	0.6
Federal credit agencies	0.3	—0.1	0.3	0.2	—0.6	0.1	0.8	0.8	0.5*
Business corporations	—5.4	—0.3	0.4	0.2	—1.0	—2.5	—1.5	—1.5	0.9*
State and local governments	0.3	0.1	1.1	1.3	0.3	2.4	2.8	—	2.0*
Foreign investors	1.0	0.4	1.9	0.6	0.8	—	—2.2	1.2	—1.5*
Individuals and others	—0.2	—0.6	1.5	1.6	3.7	1.2	2.6	—0.4	3.3
Total	$—1.8	$6.7	$8.2	$4.6	$7.0	$1.3	$2.0	$9.4	$11.0

*Estimated.
Sources: Citations in schedules, Chapters 2–6; *Federal Reserve Bulletin; Treasury Bulletin;* Bankers Trust Company, *The Investment Outlook.* Some columns do not add to totals because of rounding.

trust funds) therefore include the whole range of maturities.

Business corporations change their holdings (short maturities) with their changing need of operating cash. Liquidation to meet expansion and, in part, to avoid high interest costs is apparent in 1964 through 1968. Foreign and individuals' holdings also show cyclical variations. Among the institutional owners, commercial bank acquisitions show the greatest volatility. Bank funds move into and out of this asset with the changing cyclical demand for loans. In 1962 through 1966, net liquidation helped to meet the credit strain of those years (see Chapter 2). As we have seen, life insurance companies, mutual savings banks, and pension funds have steadily reduced their Federal investments. In contrast to their influence on the corporate bond and stock markets, institutional investors (other than commercial and Federal Reserve banks) have had a declining impact on the market for Federal debt. The steady increase in holdings by Federal Reserve banks reflects the expansion of their deposits and their contribution to the money supply in the 1960's.

Ownership of the Federal Debt

At the end of 1968 the gross direct and guaranteed debt of the Federal government was owned as shown in Table 7-5. Over two-thirds of the debt is held outside the commercial banking system. Although debt held by institutions is not demonetized in the technical sense, it is subject to only indirect fiscal influence. Nearly 40 per cent is held by Federal trust funds and by individuals; the nonmarketable character of these holdings remove them from any impact on the market. The share of debt held by business corporations and foreign investors constitutes a volatile element and exerts a more than proportional influence on yields.

The changes in the ownership of Federal obligations have resulted in an interesting pattern. We have already discussed the shifts in institutional ownership. Holdings by "other corporations" represent mainly short-term obligations held for liquidity; the amount has become very

Table 7-5. Ownership of Federal Securities, 1968, Billions of Dollars

			Per Cent
Commercial banks		$ 64.7	18.0
Federal Reserve banks		52.9	14.7
Mutual savings banks		3.8	1.6
Savings and loan associations		9.5	2.6
Life insurance companies		4.4	1.2
Property-liability insurance companies		5.4	1.5
Uninsured corporate pension funds		2.5	0.7
Federal insurance and pension funds		67.9	19.0
Federal credit agencies		3.8	1.0
Other federal agencies		4.9	1.3
Investment companies (mutual)		1.1	0.3
Other corporations		14.6	4.0
State and local government retirement funds (est.)		6.1	1.7
State and local governments (direct)		21.1	5.9
Individuals:			
Savings bonds	$51.5		
Other	23.7	75.2	20.9
Foreign and international		14.3	4.0
Miscellaneous		6.4	1.7
Total		$358.6	100

Source: *Treasury Bulletin*, adjusted for data in Chapters 2–6.

substantial. State and local government holdings represent investment of miscellaneous trust funds and liquid assets. Together with retirement funds, their share is significant. Individuals owned $24 billions of debt in addition to $51 billions of savings bonds. The latter, yielding 4¼ per cent to maturity (October 1969), have declined in attraction relative to competing savings and capital-market instruments. The Federal insurance and pension funds own special nonmarketable issues for the reserves of the insurance and retirement plans managed by the Treasury (see p. 75).

Organization of the Secondary Market

The secondary market is largely a dealer market, both for short-term maturities, which are close substitutes for money, and for the longer-term issues. Yields vary with maturity, and the dealers arbitrage the yields on various maturities to produce spreads satisfactory to the buyers and sellers of the various issues. The market is the mechanism whereby the structure of interest rates affects the flow of savings according to the demands of borrowers and lenders.

Although Federal obligations are listed on the New York Stock Exchange, transactions in outstanding securities are made in the over-the-counter market through dealers and a limited number of banks. Operations are conducted by telephone and teletype. The Federal Reserve Bank of New York also operates a trading desk for open-market operations. Some dealers specialize in certain securities. While also active in the short-term market, the larger dealers and banks do most of the trading in longer-term maturities. They keep in constant touch with the locus of ownership of different issues and with potential buyers, on a national basis. The smaller dealers tend to concentrate more in the New York market than elsewhere.

Dealers act mainly as principals for their own account, "making markets" for customers and other dealers by quoting firm prices or spreads at which they are willing to buy and sell. However, in large transactions in longer-maturity issues, the larger dealers also act as brokers. The broker function reflects the smaller size of longer-maturity issues and the frequency of Treasury refundings.

The Federal Reserve System provides important services. As we have seen, it auctions Treasury bills and acts as fiscal agent of the Treasury in the exchange of issues involved in refunding. The Federal Reserve Bank of New York is particularly active, serving as the medium for transactions of the Federal Reserve Open Market Committee with dealers. It also acts as agent for other buyers and sellers. The Federal Reserve banks also finance dealer positions through the use of repurchase agreements, which are, in effect, temporary loans.

Financial institutions, including commercial and Federal Reserve banks, are the dealers' major customers, although a growing volume of business in bills and certificates is done with corporations. The market for Federal obligations is the largest security market in the country. In 1968, the dollar volume of transactions conducted by dealers reporting to the Federal Reserve Bank of New York averaged $2½ billions per day.[1]

Prices and Yields

The yields and prices of marketable government securities rise and fall with general changes in short- and long-term interest rates, which in turn reflect the demand of and supply for funds. Because these yields represent the price of riskless money, they are close to being pure interest rates. They are however, subject to two special influences: (1) changing Treasury debt policy with respect to the issue and redemption of different maturities, and its effects, through supply, on the yield pattern; and (2) Federal Reserve policy implemented through open-market operations, which affects both supply and demand and which influences yields on different maturities through shifts in buying and selling between short- and long-term securities.

The data in Table 7-6 on the market yields (averages of daily yields) of short-, medium-, and long-term Treasury obligations for selected months show the peaks and lows in the general level of yields and the shifts in the spread among different maturities. Since 1951, yields have fluctuated in a pronounced pattern related in part to the general business cycle but more to money and capital-market conditions. In 1953 the Federal Reserve Open Market Committee began its "bills only" policy to minimize its influence on the yields and prices of long-term bonds. By October 1957, as a result of economic expansion, short- and medium-term yields had risen drastically; the latter even exceeded the long-term rate. By the middle of 1958, recession brought down the whole structure and reversed the spread. Tight money prevailed through the end of 1959, by which time short- and intermediate-term yields again exceeded the long-term (for which a maximum coupon rate of 4.25 per cent was in effect). The general decline in yields until May 1961 produced the more typical situation—yields rising with maturities.

Table 7-6. Yields on U.S. Government Securities,
Selected Dates, 1954–1969

	June 1954	Oct. 1957	June 1958	Dec. 1959	May 1961	Sept. 1966	June 1967	Nov. 1969
3-month bills	0.64	3.58	0.83	4.57	2.29	5.36	3.53	7.24
3–5-year notes and bonds	1.79	3.99	2.25	4.95	3.28	5.62	4.96	7.57
Long-term bonds	2.70	3.73	3.19	4.27	3.73	4.79	4.86	6.51

Source: *Federal Reserve Bulletin.*

[1]Source: *Federal Reserve Bulletin.*

Then came a long climb in all money and capital-market rates that culminated in the "credit crunch" in the fall of 1966. Demand for both short and long funds by individuals, corporations, governments, and institutions ran far ahead of supply and drove yields to record heights. Short-and medium-term yields substantially exceeded the long term. The process was magnified by the credit policy of the Federal Reserve, which kept the discount rate at 4½ per cent from December 1965.

Some weakening of yields until the middle of 1967 and the decline in short-term below long-term rates, encouraged by the reduction to 4 per cent in the discount rate in April 1967, reflected an easing in the money and capital markets. Then yields soared again until, by the end of 1968, they had reached all-time highs. The discount rate had been raised to 5½ per cent in December. The prime rate, at which city banks lent to their strongest customers, went to 7 per cent, and, as we shall see in subsequent chapters, yields on municipal and corporate obligations reached new heights.

The trend continued into 1969. During the first half of the year, yields on all maturities continued to rise as a new "crunch" developed. Efforts of the Federal Reserve to aid in discouraging the expansion of credit and thus to help in controlling inflation included the increase in the discount rate to 6 per cent in April, together with increases in member bank reserve requirements. In June 1969, the bank prime rate went to 8½ per cent. By December, 90-day Treasury bills were selling to yield 7.2 per cent, one-year bills 7.5 per cent, and a new issue of 18-months notes required 7¾ per cent—the highest coupon rate in 110 years. Long-term yields also set new highs. The average yield on long-term Treasurys at the end of November was 6.6 per cent. The extreme variation and erosion in the price of long-term Treasury bonds resulting from the increases in yield are indicated by the fact that whereas in July 1954, the average price of taxable Treasury's was 108, by the fall of 1969, it was at its all-time low of 62.

Securities of Federal Credit Agencies

The term *Federal agencies* covers a changing group of organizations that serve many different purposes. Our interest lies in those credit agencies whose activities in public lending and borrowing of long-term funds involve them in the capital markets. Federal credit agencies have had an important indirect influence in the capital markets. On the supply side, they have made loans to member organizations that in turn acquired capital-market instruments. On the demand side, they have borrowed from or sold stock to the Treasury and have sold stock to and acquired deposits from member organizations. Some of the funds of the member organizations have thus been diverted from direct employment in the markets.

These agencies have come directly into the primary and secondary capital markets by acquiring Federal obligations, mortgages, municipal bonds, and, to a certain extent, notes and securities of business, and by selling their own obligations to individual and institutional investors. Our attention is confined to those agencies that have been very active in the later years of the postwar period.[2]

Public Borrowing

The direct debentures and notes of the credit agencies (exclusive of the Federally guaranteed securities of the Federal Housing Administration) outstanding at the end of selected years are shown in Table 7-7.

Table 7-7. Outstanding Securities of Federal Credit Agencies, 1950–1968, Billions of Dollars

	1950	1955	1960	1965	1968
Banks for Cooperatives	$0.1	$0.1	$0.4	$ 0.8	$ 1.3
Federal Home Loan Banks	0.6	1.0	1.3	5.2	4.7
Federal Intermediate Credit Banks	0.5	0.7	1.5	2.3	3.6
Federal Land Banks	0.7	1.2	2.2	3.7	5.4
Federal National Mortgage Association	—	0.6	2.5	1.9	6.8
Tennessee Valley Authority	—	—	0.1	0.3	0.5
Total	$1.9	$3.6	$7.9	$14.1	$22.3

Sources: *Federal Reserve Bulletin; Moody's Government Manual; Treasury Bulletin.*

The public debt of Federal agencies rises and falls with the volume of their activities and with their changing reliance on debt financing. Although the total is relatively small, in some recent years the annual increases have exceeded those of government debt and have drawn substantial sums from the capital markets. The following data show the annual net changes in outstanding publicly held notes and debentures of the agencies listed in Table 7-7 from 1960 through 1968 (billions of dollars):

1960	1961	1962	1963	1964	1965	1966	1967	1968
$—	$1.1	$1.7	$1.5	$0.4	$2.0	$3.8	$—0.2	$4.0

These figures do not indicate total activity in the capital markets. Other sources have been employed, and some funds have been devoted to farm and urban loans of a specialized or short-term nature and to loans to member organizations. Therefore, the annual net public bor-

[2]Thus we exclude the Reconstruction Finance Corporation, the Federal Farm Mortgage Corporation, and The Home Owners Loan Corporation.

rowing and the annual direct investment in capital-market instruments shown in Table 7-8 are unlike. The differences between the uses and sources are included in the residual figures for "individuals and others" in the "sources" section of the master table in Chapter 12.

Chief Investments

Federal credit agencies direct funds to the capital markets mainly by acquiring Federal securities and mortgages of different types and by different routes. With the exception of the case of the Federal National Mortgage Association, much of the influence of the Federal credit agencies in the mortgage market has been indirect, through member organizations.

The chief assets of the selected credit agencies were as in Table 7-8 at selected year ends. Banks for Cooperatives make loans to farmers' cooperatives to finance the handling and packing of farm commodities. The 11 Federal Home Loan Banks advance funds to member savings and loan associations (all Federally chartered and state-chartered associations which choose to join) for mortgage loan purposes (see Chapter 3). The Federal National Mortgage Association (now privately owned) acquires FHA-insured and VA-guaranteed mortgages in both the primary and secondary markets (see Chapter 11).[3] The 12 Federal

Table 7-8. Assets of Federal Credit Agencies,
1950–1968, Billions of Dollars

	1950	1955	1960	1965	1968
Loans to co-ops	$0.3	$0.4	$0.6	$1.1	$1.6
Banks for Cooperatives:					
Federal Home Loan Banks:					
Loans to members	0.8	1.4	2.0	6.0	5.3
Federal National Mortgage Association:					
Mortgage loans	—	0.1	2.8	2.5	6.9
Federal Intermediate Credit Banks:					
Loans	0.6	0.7	1.5	2.5	3.7
Federal Land Banks:					
Mortgage Loans	0.9	1.5	2.6	4.3	6.1

Source: *Federal Reserve Bulletin.* Federal National Mortgage Association (FNMA) data cover secondary market operations only.

[3]FNMA, which is no longer classified as a Federal credit agency since it became privately owned during 1968, has also issued participation certificates representing a beneficial interest in Federally supported mortgages. The Government National Mortgage Association, which succeeded to the management and liquidation functions of FNMA, had $7.9 billions of certificates outstanding at the end of 1968. This figure was not included in agency securities outstanding (p. 97) because the mortgages supporting them are included in total mortgages (Chapters 11 and 12). The Export-Import Bank, the Commodity Credit Corporation, and the Small Business Administration have also issued participation certificates.

Intermediate Credit Banks lend on farm notes pledged by member production credit associations. The 12 Federal Land Banks provide long-term mortgage credit through local member farm credit associations.

The annual changes in the investments of Federal credit agencies in major capital-market assets from 1960 through 1968 are shown in Table 7-9.

Annual Changes in Ownership of Federal Agency Securities

The market for Federal agency securities (excluding participation certificates) is shown by the data in Table 7-10 on annual changes in ownership, 1960–1968. Individual and consolidated issues of the Federal credit agencies have virtually the same market as Federal obligations. Commercial banks and business corporations are the chief buyers of the short-term issues; the longer term are acquired by a variety of owners.

Commercial banks and business corporations have varied their net purchases with liquidity requirements. Individuals find these securities especially attractive in years of sharp decline in common stock prices such as 1962, 1966, and 1969.

Yields

Yields of agency securities follow closely those of other high-grade obligations and have usually been slightly above those of government bonds and below those of high-grade corporate bonds. Temporary changes in supply and demand produce changes in the differentials. In late December 1969, a 6.00 per cent Federal Land Bank bond due in February 1972 sold to yield 8.46 per cent, while a 4.0 per cent Treasury bond of the same maturity yielded 8.34 per cent. The high yields and the substantial spread reflected the very elevated level of general interest rates at that time.

Table 7-9. Annual Changes in Capital-Market Assets, Federal Credit Agencies, 1960–1968, Billions of Dollars

	1960	1961	1962	1963	1964	1965	1966	1967	1968*
U.S. government securities	$0.3	$—0.1	$0.3	$0.5	$—0.6	$0.1	$0.8	$0.8	$0.5
Mortgages	0.8	0.2	0.1	—1.0	0.3	0.2	2.5	1.7	2.0
Total	$1.1	$0.1	$0.4	$—0.5	$—0.3	$0.3	$3.3	$2.5	$2.5

*Estimated.
Sources: *Federal Reserve Bulletin;* Bankers Trust Company, *The Investment Outlook* (annual).

Table 7-10.   Acquisitions of Federal Credit Agency Securities,
1960–1968, Billions of Dollars

	1960	1961	1962	1963	1964	1965	1966	1967	1968
Commercial banks	$0.4	$0.7	$0.9	$0.5	$—	$1.1	$—	$0.5	$0.8
Mutual savings banks	0.1	—	0.1	0.1	0.1	—	0.2	0.2	0.4
Savings and loan associations	—	—	−0.1	0.1	0.1	0.1	0.1	0.3	0.3
Property and liability insurance companies	—	—	0.1	0.1	0.1	0.2	—	—	—
Corporate pension funds	0.1	—	—	—	—	—	—	—	−0.2
State and local government retirement funds	—	0.1	0.1	0.1	—	0.6	0.1	—	0.1
Business corporations	−0.1	0.1	—	0.2	−0.4	0.4	0.3	−1.5	—
State and local governments	—	—	0.1	—	—	—	0.1	0.5	0.8
Individuals and others	−0.6	0.2	0.6	0.4	0.4	—	3.0	−0.2	1.8
Total	—	$1.1	$1.7	$1.5	$0.4	$2.1	$3.8	$—0.2	$4.0

Sources: Bankers Trust Company, *The Investment Outlook.* Data are revised from sources indicated in Chapters 2–6, especially *Federal Reserve Bulletin* and *Treasury Bulletin.*

The Market for State and Local Government Bonds

STATE and local governments use three main types of debt: bonds sold to the public, tax anticipation notes sold to banks, and loans from the Federal government. Local governments also rely heavily on state grants. Because it is the major source, we are concerned mainly with the first category.

Bonds are typically issued in serial maturities, with designated par amounts due in successive years to final maturity. Investors have a wide choice among short-, intermediate-, and long-term maturities.

The maturity of state and local government bonds has tended to increase in recent years. Many issues of larger units run as long as 30 years and even longer when based on the revenue from specific projects. Such a trend parallels that of mortgages, whose buyers are also finding longer maturities acceptable.

With the exception of revenue bonds, the obligations of state and local governments are supported by the "full faith and credit" of taxing jurisdictions. They all (including revenue bonds) enjoy exemption of interest from Federal income taxation. This exemption gives them a special appeal to many investors, and their yields reflect the value of the exemption. Their yields are, of course, also influenced by the general supply of and demand for funds in the capital market.

101

The legal history of Federal income-tax exemption and the arguments pro and con constitute a subject too complex to discuss here.[1] It has had an enormous effect on the ability of state and local governments to attract low-cost funds to finance their great postwar expenditures for schools, highways, and other projects.

Classification of Bonds

A convenient classification of bonds combines the issuer and the degree of tax support or other means of payment:

(1) General ("full faith and credit") obligations secured by the general taxing power of governmental units
    (a) Regular:
        States
        Counties and parishes
        Cities, towns, boroughs, etc.
    (b) Special tax districts:
        School districts
        Water districts
        Etc.
(2) Revenue bonds (nonguaranteed) secured only by special income
    (a) Municipal utilities departments, etc.
    (b) Quasimunicipal authorities and commissions
    (c) Regular governmental units supporting the issue from special taxes only or from project income
(3) Housing authority issues further supported by state or Federal guarantee of principal and interest (a special type of revenue bond)

Bonds can also be classified as to quality. Securities bond-rating services rate full faith and credit obligations of states from Baa to Aaa; local government bonds and revenue bonds show a range from those in default to Aaa. Some local municipalities have higher ratings than some states do.

Regular governmental units possess broad general powers of taxation, limited only by statute with respect to types of taxes, total general debt in relation to property value, and limitations on the property tax rate. They ordinarily pledge their general credit but may also pledge specific revenues. Special districts, organized to operate a specific activity such as schools, also have the power to tax the property within their borders. Revenue bonds are issued by states, counties, and local units payable from some specific source, and by departments and statutory

---

[1] See Lucille Derrick, *Exemption of Security Interest from Income Taxes in the United States;* in *Journal of Business,* October, 1946, Part 2, Chap. 3; D. J. Ott and A. H. Meltzer, *Federal Tax Treatment of State and Local Securities* (Washington, D.C.: The Brookings Institution, 1963).

authorities (quasi-public corporations without the power to tax) organized to operate revenue-producing projects.

Growth and Types of State and Local Debt

Table 1-2 shows that in the postwar period the rate of growth of state and local government debt has far outstripped that of the Federal government. This growth reflects the expansion of governmental services and the growth of population and its steady urbanization. The growth of state and local debt in relation to Federal debt is also revealed by figures of year-end per capita debt.[2]

	1950	1955	1960	1965	1968
Direct Federal gross debt	$1,697	$1,662	$1,591	$1,631	$1,774
State and local gross debt	159	268	389	513	(est.) 638

As of January 1967, there were over 81,000 governmental units in the United States, including states, counties, cities, towns, and other municipalities, and special tax districts.[3] Possibly 20,000 of those have borrowed through the sale of bonds. The number of outstanding issues was estimated at 25,000 for 1950;[4] it is certainly considerably higher today.

Table 8-1 shows the composition of state and local debt by major types for selected years (as of June 30). Net debt is after deductions for sinking fund.

Revenue bonds have increased much more than general obligations,

Table 8-1. Outstanding Debt of State and Local Governments, 1950–1968, as of June 30, Billions of Dollars

	1950	1955	1960	1965	1968
Long-term debt:					
Full faith and credit	$19.9	$30.5	$41.7	$56.4	$65.1
Nonguaranteed	3.1	11.8	25.1	37.8	47.6
	$23.0	$42.3	$66.8	$94.2	$112.7
Short-term debt	1.1	2.0	3.2	5.3	8.4
Total debt	$24.1	$44.3	$70.0	$99.5	$121.1
Net long-term debt	$20.7	$38.4	$61.6	$86.0	$104.0

Sources: U.S. Department of Commerce, Bureau of the Census, *Governmental Finances* (annual).

[2]Sources: U.S. Department of Commerce, Bureau of the Census, *Statistical Abstract of the United States* and *Governmental Finances* (annual).

[3]U.S. Department of Commerce, Bureau of the Census, *1967 Census of Governments, Governmental Organization.*

[4]Irwin Friend, *et al., Over-the-Counter Securities Markets* (New York: McGraw-Hill Book Company, 1958), p. 54.

reflecting the growth of municipal departments and of special commissions and authorities to operate utility, toll-road, airport, bridge, and other facilities. Authorities are sponsored by both state and local governments and in some cases jointly by two or more jurisdictions. At the end of 1968, nonguaranteed bonds constituted over 40 per cent of total "municipal" long-term bonds outstanding (as contrasted with less than 14 per cent in 1950); 40 per cent of all new bonds issued in 1968 were of this type.[5] Use of revenue rather than direct borrowing avoids the statutory limits on "full faith and credit" debt and the legal restrictions on purposes for which tax revenues can be employed. The outstanding long-term debt as of June 30, 1968, by governmental unit, is shown in Table 8-2.

Purposes of Borrowing

Long-term debt is issued to meet special operating expenses, to finance capital project construction not borne by current revenues or grants from the Federal and other governments, and to refund maturing obligations. Although there is no exact relationship between the amount of debt financing and capital expenditures, most of the debt anticipates, then funds, part of the capital cost of projects involving fixed assets.[6]

The term *part of the cost* is used because, in recent years, the annual increase in long-term debt has been only about one-third of capital outlay expenditures and an even smaller proportion of actual construction costs. Much capital construction by governments is financed from general and special tax revenues—for example, the use of gasoline taxes for highway construction. Revenue bonds financing of self-supporting departments and authorities tends to follow more precisely the capital cost of their enterprises. The data in Table 8-3 show the purposes of long-term debt outstanding (both direct and unguaranteed) as of June

Table 8-2.   Long-Term State and Local Debt, 1968, Billions of Dollars

	Full Faith and Credit	Nonguaranteed	Total
States	$14.7	$18.9	$33.6
Counties	6.9	1.6	8.5
Municipalities (cities)	20.2	13.7	33.9
Townships	1.9	0.1	2.0
School districts	18.0	—	18.0
Special districts	3.4	13.3	16.7
Total	$65.1	$47.6	$112.7

Source: U.S. Department of Commerce, Bureau of the Census, *Governmental Finances in 1967–1968.*

[5]*Federal Reserve Bulletin.*

[6]In recent years, Federal funds have financed about 20 per cent of state and local public construction through loans and grants.

Table 8-3.   Purposes of State and Local Long-Term Debt,
1962, Billions of Dollars

Table 8–3.	State	Per Cent	Local	Per Cent	Total	Per Cent
Education	$ 4.0	18.6	$19.0	34.1	$23.0	29.8
Highways	9.6	44.8	4.1	7.4	13.7	17.8
Local utilities	—	—	12.6	22.5	12.6	16.3
Sewerage	—	—	5.3	9.5	5.3	6.9
Housing and urban renewal	0.6	3.1	4.6	8.2	5.2	6.7
Hospitals	0.3	1.2	1.0	1.7	1.3	1.6
Airports	—	—	1.2	2.1	1.2	1.5
Port and terminal facilities	0.3	1.5	0.8	1.3	1.1	1.4
Veterans' bonuses	0.9	4.3	—	—	0.9	1.2
Other	5.7	26.5	7.3	13.2	13.0	16.8
Total	$21.4	100	$55.9	100	$77.3	100

U.S. Department of Commerce, Bureau of the Census, *1962 Census of Governments, Long-Term Debt of State and Local Governments*, Preliminary Report Number 7 (December 1962). *Federal Reserve Bulletin* reports the purposes of issues for new capital on an annual basis.

30, 1962. The data reveal the relative importance of various functions of states as compared with those of local governments. All categories have shared in the sharp increase in outstanding debt in recent years.

Organization of the Primary Market

The first step in the issuance of a new state or local government bond issue is its authorization by the governmental unit under the terms of the prevailing statute. The financial officer then determines the terms of the issue—denominations, interest rate, serial maturities, etc.—and advertises it for sale under competitive bidding, ordinarily in the *Daily Bond Buyer*. The chief buyers are large investment banking firms, some of which specialize in such securities, and commercial banks, which are authorized to act as underwriters of municipal issues (general obligations only).[7] Less than 60 large banks are active in the market for large new issues. Some banks, even large ones, confine their holdings to bonds of issuers within their state. Smaller issues tend to be purchased by local banks.

In most states, individual underwriters or syndicates must acquire general obligations by competitive bidding. Competitive bidding is expected to produce lower yields than negotiation; it does, however, deprive the issuer of the initial advice and continuous services of the investment banker. Revenue bonds are frequently sold on a negotiated basis; their more specialized nature and generally lower quality make the aid of a banker in consulation and tailoring of features more necessary.

Buying syndicates are managed by firms which invite other banks

[7] Public Housing Administration bonds are the exception.

and dealers to participate in the underwriting. The larger underwritings are managed by a limited number of banks or firms, and underwriters often specialize in issues from a particular area or in certain types of obligations.

Bidding for municipal bonds (and their later resale) is on a yield basis on bids of par value or more. The syndicate determines the yields at which the various serial maturities will be absorbed, then adds a gross spread to cover buying risk and distribution expense. Some invitations to bid require that all maturities bear the same coupon rate; in other cases the coupon may vary with maturity. Under the former arrangement, the offering price is adjusted above par for the different serial blocks because the market ordinarily requires that yields rise with length to maturity. Where the coupon varies with maturity, the rate may be set very high on early maturities, and these are resold at substantial premiums.

The gross underwriting spread, or difference between cost and offering price, is the margin within which the successful bidder must be prepared to work. It ranges from less than 1 to 1.5 per cent (with the average around 1 per cent) and is a function of type, size, quality, marketability, and maturity.

The successful individual bidder or syndicate may retain the issue for its own inventory (as banks do for investment), retail it to its own customers, or reoffer it to dealers at a modest concession from the public offering price. Both in the original bidding and in later trading, the prices of the various maturities are indicated in terms of yield rather than in dollars.

Postwar Volume and Buyers of New Municipal Securities

In recent years a fairly steady increase in municipal financing has resulted from the expansion of governmental services and the favorable market for "tax-exempt" securities. The data in Table 8-4 show the gross proceeds (at time of delivery) of new long-term issues, including

Table 8-4.   Borrowing by State and Local Governments, 1960–1968, Billions of Dollars

	1960	1961	1962	1963	1964	1965	1966	1967	1968
New capital issues	$7.2	$8.4	$8.6	$10.1	$10.5	$11.1	$11.1	$14.3	$16.4
Less—refunding and refinancing	3.8	3.9	4.0	3.9	5.2	5.0	5.6	6.9	5.3
	3.5	4.5	4.6	6.2	5.3	6.1	5.5	8.4	11.1
Federal loans and other debt	0.3	0.7	1.0	0.9	0.9	1.7	1.2	2.1	0.6
Increase in debt	$3.8	$5.2	$5.6	$7.1	$6.2	$7.8	$6.7	$10.5	$11.4

Sources: Investment Bankers Association of America, *Statistical Bulletin;* Bankers Trust Company, *The Investment Outlook* (annual); *Federal Reserve Bulletin,* including flow-of-funds tables.

those issues placed with state and local government retirement funds. These proceeds are reduced to the net annual increase by deducting refinancing and retirements. Increases in loans from the Federal government are added to produce the annual volume of total new debt.

The data reveal a secular increase in financing and some cyclical variation. In periods of tight money such as 1966, 1968, and 1969, characterized by rising yields and lower bond prices, a considerable amount of planned financing was withdrawn or postponed. During recession years like 1961, when lower yields prevail, financing is sometimes increased. (The low rate in 1960 is attributable to the carry-over of the effects of the previous 2 years.) The upward course resumed in 1961 through 1963 reflected increased public construction expenditures. The practice of advanced refundings, or sale of bonds to refund issues due possibly several years in the future (with the proceeds being temporarily invested), inflates the new issue figures in some years such as 1963 and 1967.

In 1969 the high cost of funds, threats against the tax-free status of bond income, and statutory ceilings on municipal bond coupon rates reduced borrowing substantially and caused deferment of many capital projects.

New issues are absorbed primarily by taxed institutions, especially commercial banks, which not only underwrite but also invest (except in revenue bonds) for their own account. Some bonds are placed with government retirement funds (see Chapter 5), and a modest amount with state and local governments proper and business corporations. Individuals seeking tax relief account for most of the balance. The data in Table 8-5 show the annual net changes in ownership since 1960.

Variations in annual net acquisitions by investors are only partly

Table 8-5. Annual Acquisitions of State and Local Government Bonds, 1960–1968, Billions of Dollars

	1960	1961	1962	1963	1964	1965	1966	1967	1968
Commercial banks	$0.6	$2.8	$4.4	$5.0	$3.8	$5.1	$2.4	$9.0	$8.1
Mutual savings banks	—	—	−0.2	−0.1	—	−0.1	−0.1	—	—
Life insurance companies	0.4	0.3	0.1	−0.2	−0.1	−0.2	−0.4	−0.1	—
Property insurance companies	1.0	0.9	0.6	0.7	0.3	0.2	0.7	1.5	1.1
State and local government retirement funds	0.2	0.1	−0.4	−0.4	−0.5	−0.3	−0.1	−0.1	−0.1
Business corporations	−0.1	−0.2	0.2	0.9	0.2	0.7	0.8	0.7	0.1*
State and local governments	−0.1	0.1	−0.3	−0.3	−0.1	−0.1	−0.1	—	−0.2*
Individuals and others	1.8	1.2	1.2	1.5	2.5	2.5	3.5	−0.5	2.5*
Total	$3.8	$5.2	$5.6	$7.1	$6.2	$7.8	$6.7	$10.5	$11.4

*Estimated.
Sources: See citations in schedules, Chapters 2–6; Bankers Trust Company, *The Investment Outlook* (annual). Some columns do not add to totals because of rounding.

explained by changes in their available funds. Individuals, and especially institutions, switch in and out of municipals as the relative yields on competive investments rise and fall. Bank acquisitions show the greatest variations in a loose cyclical pattern. Changes in their reserve position and in the demand for loans, which they prefer, determine their holdings and purchases of these securities. This situation is well illustrated by the drop in acquisition of municipals in 1966 and by the rebound to record acquisitions in 1967 and 1968. Bank policy was also affected by the influx of savings deposits in 1962, 1963, and 1967, part of which was invested in municipal bonds for their advantageous after-tax yields (see Chapter 2). These bonds are even more attractive now that rates paid on savings have increased.

The interest of life insurance companies in municipal bonds was stimulated by the increase in their income-tax rate in 1959. In recent years, however, their rate of acquisition of tax exempts has declined in favor of greater mortgage commitments. Property and liability insurance companies, whose investment income is fully taxed, showed increasing annual acquisitions until 1960 and 1961: common stocks had more appeal in more recent years until 1967 and 1968, when tax exempts again came into favor. State and local government retirement funds have reduced their investment in tax-exempt bonds. These funds are not taxed, and other securities offer more attractive yields (see Chapter 6).

Variations in acquisitions by business corporations and individuals are more difficult to explain. Some countercyclical pattern in net purchases is evident, explained possibly by variations in total savings and by the fact that in years of rapidly rising prices of common stocks, the latter become relatively attractive for capital gains. Indeed, the higher the income bracket, the less individuals may be interested in current income, substantial though the after-tax rate from municipals may be.

Ownership of State and Local Government Bonds

At the end of 1968, the estimated ownership schedule was as shown in Table 8-6. The last category, individuals and others, includes partnerships, bank trust accounts, savings and loan associations, dealers and brokers, and foreign owners. Individual ownership, direct and through trusts, probably accounts for 90 per cent of the figure.

Organization of the Secondary Market

Individual and institutional investors in tax-exempt bonds require a good secondary market when orderly liquidation of their holdings becomes necessary. Trading is done by the original underwriting firms and banks and by dealers who specialize in these securities in the over-the-counter market. The secondary and primary marketing or-

Table 8-6.   Ownership of State and Local Government Bonds,
1968, Billions of Dollars

		Per Cent
Commercial banks	$58.7	46.0
Mutual savings banks	0.2	0.2
Life insurance companies	3.2	2.5
Property insurance companies	14.4	11.2
State and local government retirement funds*	2.3	1.8
State and local governments*	2.2	1.7
Business corporations*	5.2	4.0
Individuals and others (residual)	41.8	32.6
Total	$128.0	100

*Estimated.
Sources: Secretary of the Treasury, *Annual Report*, adjusted to year end and for data cited in Chapters 2–6. See also *Federal Reserve Bulletin*, annual flow-of-funds tables.

ganizations consist largely of the same types of firms. The daily *Blue List of Current Municipal Offerings* may list 2,000–3,000 available issues. Although no firm data are available, the interdealer volume of transactions is known to be substantial. Although no good information on the total volume of trading exists, it is probably much lower than the volume of new offerings. However, with annual gross financing of over $16 billions and with a total of over $128 billions outstanding, even a modest turnover of the latter may eventually produce a volume equal to the new issue volume.

Yields

The yields on state and local government bonds as a class are a function of (1) interest rates in general; (2) the value to investors of the tax-exempt privilege; (3) the supply of new and outstanding securities of this type; (4) the supply of funds available for purchase of such investments; and (5) the appeal of alternative investments. Yields on individual issues are further affected by their size, quality, maturity, and marketability. Tax-exempt yields have fluctuated in a wider range than have other high-grade yields, mainly because of changes in supply in relation to that of Federal bonds, and in bank demand. The market for tax-exempt bonds is more restricted than that of Federal and corporate debt and is consequently more erratic. The data in Table 8-7 for 1955 through 1969 show the annual average yields for Moody's U. S. Treasury long-term bond series compared with Moody's Aaa and Baa state and local government bonds series. The annual averages disguise the widest variations but are suitable for our purpose. Although all yields rose and fell in a common pattern, the spread between the yield on long-term Treasury bonds and the Aaa state and local government series has shown considerable variation.

From 1955 through 1957, the supply of total investable funds re-

Table 8-7.   U.S. Government and Municipal Bond Yields, 1955–1969

	Long-Term Treasury (1)	State and Local Government		Spread (1) over (2)	Spread (3) over (2)
		(2)	(3)		
		Aaa	Baa		
1955	2.84	2.18	3.14	0.66	0.96
1956	3.08	2.51	3.50	0.57	0.99
1957	3.47	3.10	4.20	0.37	1.10
1958	3.43	2.92	3.95	0.51	1.03
1959	4.07	3.35	4.24	0.72	0.89
1960	4.01	3.26	4.22	0.75	0.96
1961	3.90	3.27	4.01	0.63	0.74
1962	3.95	3.03	3.67	0.92	0.64
1963	4.00	3.06	3.58	0.94	0.52
1964	4.15	3.09	3.54	1.06	0.45
1965	4.21	3.16	3.57	1.05	0.41
1966	4.65	3.67	4.21	0.98	0.54
1967	4.85	3.74	4.30	1.11	0.56
1968	5.26	4.20	4.88	1.06	0.68
1969*	6.05	5.35	6.00	0.70	0.65

*Eleven months.

mained fairly level in the face of demand for financing in all sectors, and yields rose sharply, culminating in "tight money" levels in the latter part of 1957. State and local government financing outran that of the Treasury, and this demand, together with a relative lack of demand on the part of banks, drove tax-free yields to the point where the spread became unusually thin.

In the recession year of 1958, all yields declined. The volume of new Federal financing remained about level, and, with the supply of funds high and with banks seeking outlets for funds not needed for loans, prices of municipal bonds were bid up and their yields dropped. A quite normal spread was produced. In 1959 there was a sharp rise in all yields, culminating in "tight money" late in the year. The increase in Federal financing caused yields on government bonds to rise more than those on tax exempts, and the spread increased substantially even though banks found business loans more attractive.

The modest increase in yields on Treasury bonds beginning in 1962 was accompanied by smaller increases in yields on high-grade municipals, so that by 1964 and 1965 the yield spread had widened to over 100 basis points. Then in 1966 came the "credit crunch," which saw all yields setting record levels. Pressure for loan funds reduced bank investment in municipals in 1966, but as the rise in yields continued, banks became aggressive buyers in 1966 and 1967. The lessening pressure in the corporate market that produced somewhat lower yields was not experienced in either the long-term government or municipals market in 1967. Yields continued to rise and in November 1969 the 6.3 per cent yield on the composite group far surpassed previous levels. All elements of demand in the bond market sought an increasing share of a diminishing supply of funds.

The high level of market yields posed a problem. In many states statutory limits on state bond coupons (for example, 5 per cent in California) are lower than required yields. Therefore, much new long-term financing was virtually stopped in 1969.

The drastic rise in the yields on municipal bonds produced a concomitant decline in their price. Standard & Poor's price index for a 4-per cent 20-year bond stood at 123 (average) in 1955. By December 1969 it was 69. Such price erosion contributed substantially to the credit crisis in 1969; banks could not switch funds from long-term municipal bonds to loans without realizing very substantial losses.

The spread between taxable and tax-free yields is the price investors are willing to pay for the privilege of tax exemption. This price changes with the general level of yields and with the changing constituency of buyers. The continuing high spread in the latter 1960's reflected high general yields, higher income taxes, and increased numbers of investors seeking tax relief.

The yield curve for state and local bonds has not been shaped like that for Treasury obligations (see Chapter 7). Longer maturities produce substantially higher rates. For example, late in September, 1969, Aaa-rated 20-year general obligations bore an average yield of 5.75 per cent, while 5-year maturities sold to yield 5.30 per cent and 1-year maturities, 5.10 per cent. In the same month, yields on Treasury obligations of similar maturities were 6.30, 7.50, and 7.65 per cent, respectively. The chief buyers of municipal bonds, commercial banks, now greatly prefer short- and intermediate-term obligations. The longer terms have their chief appeal to individual investors.

Yields on individual municipal issues are also a function of quality, size, and marketability. Quality tends to correlate roughly with size— the big name issues finding the best market. The previous data reveal, however, that the differential of Baa over Aaa yields has been declining steadily until recent years. As the tax-free privilege became more valuable to more investors, they were willing to accept a lower premium on lesser-grade issues. However, the hectic pressure for funds in 1966 through 1969 drove all yields to record heights, and investors began to require a higher spread on lesser-grade obligations.

The Market for Long-Term Corporate Debt

Definitions and Reasons for Use

OUR definition of the capital markets as the markets for funds of over 1 year in maturity suggests a rather broad definition of corporate intermediate- and long-term debt. It includes longer-term trade payables, mortgages, term loans, corporate 1–5-year notes sold in the open market, and corporate bonds. Because precise data on some of these categories are lacking and because we are interested mainly in debt whose yields are determined in open competition, attention is confined to corporate term loans and bonds.

Term loans are business debts with more than 1 year maturity, negotiated directly with banks and insurance companies and ordinarily amortized on a serial basis. They are used to finance both working capital and fixed-asset requirements, and the repayment schedule is related to the future cash flow of the borrower. The latest available data on the volume of bank term lending are shown on p. 17. Insurance companies class their term loans as "industrial and miscellaneous" bonds, or as mortgages, and do not report separate figures for this investment.

Corporations issue bonds for a variety of reasons. The most important of these are to reduce the cost of financing and to increase the rate of return on total capital by applying the principle of leverage. The cost of borrowed long-term capital is believed to be often substantially lower than that of equity capital, especially on an after-tax basis, because interest is an expense for income-tax purposes. Bond financing also avoids possible dilution of control. Management temperament is also a major factor determining the pattern of business financing. There is often a resistance to borrowing that may be based on rational risk avoidance or simply on innate conservatism. In regulated industries, limits to borrowing are imposed by the controlling commissions. For all companies, investors' standards with respect to appropriate debt burden have, of course, a powerful influence.

General Corporate Financing

Sources of corporate funds for selected years in the postwar period are indicated at this point as a prelude to the more detailed study of corporate bond and stock markets in this and the following chapter. The emphasis is on the latter part of the period. The data in Table 9-1 summarize the net financing of non-farm, non-financial corporations (excluding banks, insurance companies, and investment companies), after eliminating trade payables to avoid double-counting. The data do not represent the total volume of actual capital-market activity because they exclude refinancing and redemptions.

Internal sources of funds predominated in each year. But although such funds are placed directly in corporate assets, they nevertheless affect the capital markets. To the extent that corporations can finance

Table 9-1.   Sources of Corporate Funds, 1950–1968, Billions of Dollars

	1950	1955	1960	1965	1966	1967	1968
Internal sources:							
Retained profits	$14.3	$13.9	$10.0	$23.1	$24.7	$21.2	$22.0
Depreciation and depletion	8.6	17.0	24.2	35.2	38.2	41.2	44.3
Inventory valuation	−5.0	−1.7	0.2	−1.7	−1.8	−1.1	−3.2
	17.9	29.2	34.4	56.6	61.2	61.2	63.1
External sources:							
Bonds	1.6	2.8	3.5	5.4	10.2	14.7	12.9
Bank term loans (est.)	0.5	0.4	0.1	2.0	2.3	1.5	4.6
Mortgages	0.6	0.7	0.7	3.9	4.2	4.5	5.8
Stocks	1.4	1.9	1.6	−	1.2	2.3	−0.8
Bank and other debt (mainly short term)	10.8	10.0	3.9	16.1	14.2	7.4	19.1
	14.9	15.8	9.8	27.4	32.1	30.4	41.6
Total sources	$32.8	$45.0	$44.2	$84.0	$93.3	$91.6	$104.7

Sources: *Survey of Current Business;* term loan data from Bankers Trust Company, *The Investment Outlook* (annual).

their needs in this manner, fewer securities and other outside financing need be used.

Variations among the long-term external sources reflect the economic outlook and the relative costs of alternative forms of financing. The relatively stable volume of bond financing in the early 1960's reflected the stability of interest rates and other factors discussed later in this chapter. Corporations stepped up their long-term borrowing very substantially in 1966 through 1968 and in so doing contributed to the tremendous total demand for long-term funds that resulted in the unprecedented interest yields that characterized those years. Stock financing is heavily influenced by the general level of stock prices (as in 1965 through 1967) and by other factors to be discussed in Chapter 10. The growing use of term loans and mortgage debt should be noted.

Outstanding Long-Term Corporate Debt

Measurements of total long- and intermediate-term corporate debt outstanding differ widely. The data on long-term debt presented in Table 1-2 are all-inclusive, covering all corporations and all debt with more than 1 year to maturity. The more refined figures of corporate bonded debt outstanding as reported regularly by the Federal Reserve are useful in a capital-market study. Data for selected years in the postwar period are shown in Table 9-2.

The steady increase in bonds outstanding (averaging $9 billions a year in the 1960's) reflects the pace of economic growth in the postwar period, the rise in prices, and the growing willingness of corporations to borrow and so save on income taxes. Fluctuations reflect variations in the pattern of corporate expenditures, mainly for fixed assets, as well as capital cost conditions in the competitive capital markets.

Public Distribution of Bonds in the Primary Market

Public issues of corporate bonds are distributed through investment banking houses. These merchants investigate and buy (underwrite) bond issues for resale to institutions and individual investors. The investment banker provides the issuer with advice on the form, timing,

Table 9-2. Domestic Corporate Bonds Outstanding, at Year End, 1950–1968, Billions of Dollars

	1950	1955	1960	1965	1968
Nonfinancial corporations	$35.7	$52.8	$74.9	$97.8	$135.9
Financial corporations	1.7	5.4	9.9	7.7	20.7
Total	$37.4	$58.2	$84.8	$115.5	$156.6

Source: *Federal Reserve Bulletin*, flow-of-funds tables.

and pricing of bond financing and with continuing counsel after the issue is floated. The banker's check on the financial condition of the issuer, the form and terms of the financing, and the maintenance of a continuous market, and his general investment information and advice are valuable to the investor. By screening issues and influencing their timing and yields, the investment banker plays a major role in the primary bond market.

Formerly called "bond houses," the larger investment banking firms engage in a variety of ancillary activities. Some serve as securities brokers and dealers and as underwriters of stock issues. In the flotation of new issues, some investment bankers are wholesalers, doing the original underwriting and then selling to retail dealers for wider distribution. Others serve also as distributors to the general investment public. Some are national in their operations; others are local. About 50 firms originate and manage the major issues of securities; many hundreds of others are involved in the final sale of the larger flotations.

Investment banking firms acquire new corporate bond issues by either negotiated or competitive bidding. Direct negotiation between issuer and underwriter (acting alone or as the manager of a syndicate) ends in a purchase contract whereby the banker, or a purchase syndicate in the case of larger flotations, acquires the issue at a net price and yield determined by bargaining. Such underwriting is largely confined to industrial and financial offerings. Competitive bidding, in which the issuer invites sealed bids of price or yield or both on an issue whose terms are already determined, is ordinarily required by Federal or state statute in the case of public utility and railroad issues. Regardless of the process of acquisition, the final purchase takes the form of a firm commitment.

Two other arrangements sometimes used do not involve total underwriting: (1) "best efforts," or agency selling, whereby the underwriter(s) agrees simply to merchandise the securities at the issuer's risk; this arrangement is used primarily in common stock rather than in bond offerings; (2) "stand-by" underwriting of convertible bonds; this method involves the guarantee of funds to the issuer from an offering of such bonds by the corporation by privileged subscription to existing stock holders; here the underwriter agrees to take up only the securities not bought through the exercise of rights.

The public offering of corporate bonds in interstate commerce or through the mails is subject to the registration and prospectus requirements of the Securities Act of 1933, save for railroad issues, which are controlled by the Interstate Commerce Commission. State "blue-sky" laws apply to intrastate offerings.

The costs of flotation of fully underwritten public issues consist of the banker's gross spread or commission and the expenses of preparation and registration. The former component varies with the size and quality of the issue and the method of distribution. It ranges between 0.5 and 8 per cent.

Direct, or Private, Placement of Bonds

A notable development in the postwar period has been the substantial growth of private placement of bonds with institutions, mostly life insurance companies (see Chapter 4) but also some commercial banks, pension funds, and investment companies. Industrial bonds predominate in such direct sales because railroad and many utility bonds must be sold under competitive bidding. Direct placements avoid the investment banking machinery save for those cases in which investment bankers act as finders or agents at a modest fee (0.25–2 per cent). Corporate bonds offerings for cash (for both new money and refinancing) from 1955 through 1968 were as shown in Table 9-3.

Private placements offer several advantages to the corporation. They reduce the risks of delay involved in registered public offerings, save on costs of flotation (except for any finder's fee), make the funds available sooner, and permit the tailoring of each loan indenture to the particular situation. Smaller corporations find such financing a substitute for bond issues they would have difficulty selling in the open market.

It is interesting to note the declining percentage of private placements since 1964, especially in 1967 and 1968. Life insurance companies, which provide the chief demand for corporate debt placed in this way, have been looking more to the higher yields available on mort-

Table 9-3.   Publicly and Privately Offered Bonds, 1955–1968, Billions of Dollars

	Publicly Offered	Privately Placed	Total	Privately Placed Per Cent
1955	$4.1	$3.3	$7.4	45
1956	4.2	3.8	8.0	47
1957	6.1	3.8	10.0	38
1958	6.3	3.3	9.7	35
1959	3.6	3.6	7.2	50
1960	4.8	3.3	8.1	41
1961	4.7	4.7	9.4	50
1962	4.5	4.5	9.0	50
1963	4.7	6.2	10.9	57
1964	3.6	7.2	10.8	67
1965	5.6	8.1	13.7	60
1966	8.0	7.5	15.5	48
1967	15.0	7.0	22.0	32
1968	9.8	6.1	15.9	38

Sources: Securities and Exchange Commission, *Annual Reports; Federal Reserve Bulletin.*

gages in recent years and have also seen an increasing share of their investable funds tied up in policy loans and common stocks (as we saw in Chapter 4). In addition, in 1967, high interest rates and nonrefunding or postponed call provisions substantially encouraged public versus private sales. In 1968, the total volume of bond financing fell off somewhat, reflecting the high level of bond interest rates, and the proportion of private sales rose moderately. But in 1969 private placements suffered from the shrinkage in life insurance company funds available for use in the capital market.

Volume and Buyers of New Bond Issues

The data in Table 9-3 show the gross proceeds of all corporate bond issues regardless of purpose, including new money and refinancing of bonds and other securities. The *net* change in outstanding corporate bonds is shown in the acquisition figures in Table 9-4. Annual variations in demand for bonds by investors reflect conditions and policies discussed in Chapters 2–6.

The data in Table 9-4 on annual net acquisitions of corporate bonds from 1960 to 1968 cumulate the figures presented in Chapters 2–6. Until

Table 9-4. Annual Net Acquisitions of Corporate Bonds, at Year End, 1960–1968, Billions of Dollars

	1960	1961	1962	1963	1964	1965	1966	1967	1968
Commercial banks	$—0.2	$—0.2	$ —	$ —	$0.2	$—0.1	$0.1	$ —	$ —
Mutual savings banks	0.1	—0.1	—	—0.2	—0.2	—0.1	0.3	1.9	1.3
Life insurance companies	1.4	2.0	1.8	2.1	1.9	2.4	2.2	3.7	3.6
Property and liability insurance companies	0.1	—	—	—0.1	0.3	0.6	0.6	0.6	1.0
Corporate pension funds	1.6	1.2	1.2	1.5	1.6	1.5	1.9	1.0	0.7
State and local government retirement funds	1.1	1.3	2.0	1.9	2.1	2.0	2.5	2.6	3.1
Investment companies	0.2	0.3	0.2	0.1	0.3	0.4	0.4	0.1	0.6
State and local governments	0.1	0.4	0.2	0.6	0.3	0.2	0.4	1.1	1.0*
Foreign investors	0.1	—0.1	—0.1	—	0.2	—0.2	0.2	—0.3	—0.3*
Individuals and others	0.5	0.3	—0.5	—0.4	—0.1	1.4	2.5	5.1	3.0*
Total	$5.0	$5.1	$4.8	$5.5	$6.6	$8.1	$11.1	$15.8	$14.0

*Estimated.
Sources: See citations in schedules, Chapters 2–6; *Federal Reserve Bulletin;* Bankers Trust Company, *The Investment Outlook* (annual); Securities and Exchange Commission, *Statistical Bulletin.*

very recent years, almost all the net increases have gone to institutions rather than to individuals. The latter were relatively disinterested because the yields on corporate bonds, especially high grade, were, until 1966 and 1967, not attractive compared with the rates available on savings investments. The great rise in bond yields in 1967 through 1969, however, has resulted in a renewed interest in corporate bonds, and the amount absorbed by the "individuals and others" category has been substantial. This category, however, includes minor institutions such as fraternal life insurance companies and foundations and endowments, as well as bank trust departments. The growing investment of state and local government retirement funds and the somewhat declining interest on the part of pension funds were noted in Chapter 5.

At the end of 1968, domestic corporate bonds were owned as shown in Table 9-5. Institutions predominate in the ownership of corporate bonds, with life insurance companies accounting for 44 per cent of the total. As we have seen (Chapter 4), life insurance companies find bonds, with their definite yields, attractive because their chief investment obligation, from the standpoint of income, is to earn the assumed rate at which reserves are compounded. Corporate pension fund investment in bonds remains significant, although these instruments constitute a steadily declining proportion of their total assets because of the greater relative increase in common stocks (Chapter 5). State and local government retirement funds have been substituting corporate for municipal bonds. The holdings of mutual investment companies, although growing at a modest rate, remain unimportant. These holdings comprise the bond investments of balanced and income funds and of a few funds devoted exclusively to bond portfolios.

Bond Trading in the Secondary Market

Because of the institutional ownership of corporate bonds, the secondary market activity in these bonds is small, especially for high-grade

Table 9-5.   Ownership of Corporate Bonds, 1968, Billions of Dollars

Commercial banks	$ 1.8
Mutual savings banks	6.6
Life insurance companies	68.5
Property and liability insurance companies	5.0
Uninsured corporate pension funds	21.1
State and local government retirement funds	23.4*
Mutual investment companies	3.4
Individuals and others	26.8*
Total	$156.6

*Estimated.
  Sources: *Federal Reserve Bulletin* (flow-of-funds tables) and data on institutional investments, Chapters 2–6.

issues. Most trading occurs in the over-the-counter market. The New York Stock Exchange constitutes virtually the entire listed market, with 1,455 issues listed at the end of 1968. The market value of domestic corporate bonds listed on the Big Board was $39 billions; bonds of foreign companies added another $600 millions.[1] These figures mean that corporate bonds with market value of approximately $117 billions were traded over the counter.

Of the thousands of unlisted corporate bond issues, probably fewer than 500 are traded on the over-the-counter market in a typical day. The majority are only occasionally transferred. Even so, about 80 per cent of corporate bond resales, or approximately $15 to $16 billions a year, take place in the "off board" rather than on the organized exchanges. The transactions are handled by broker dealers, mainly the members of the National Association of Securities Dealers. A high concentration of the actual resales are in New York. Only a handful of houses make continuous markets, but the narrow spread between the bid and asked prices of high-grade unlisted issues suggests that buyers and sellers do not suffer from a thin market.

At the end of 1968, 1,142 bond issues of American corporations were listed on the New York Stock Exchange. Of this total, fewer than 100 were actively traded. The sales of listed bonds in 1968 totaled $5.7 billions, or over 80 per cent of all listed trading in such securities.[2]

Data on changes in corporate bonds outstanding, listings on exchanges, and trading are increasingly influenced by the growing volume of convertible bonds. These securities, while bonds in name, are convertible into common shares at predetermined ratios and are, in effect, calls on common stock at a fixed price. The volume issued and traded is in part a function of the course of the stock market. From 1965 through 1968, convertible bonds constituted nearly 20 per cent of all new corporate bonds offered. In 1968, 43 of the 50 most actively traded bonds on the New York Stock Exchange were convertibles.[3]

Yields

The factors determining interest rates in the capital markets and the interrelations among rates on different instruments have been previously discussed and will be summarized in Chapter 12. We comment here on the historical pattern of corporate bond yields.

Bond yields, as one important long-term rate, change through time as long-term interest rates in general rise and fall. The spread between yields on straight corporate bonds and on Treasury bonds of like maturities represents the margin required by investors to compensate for the risk of default. It also reflects the relatively poor marketability

[1]New York Stock Exchange, *Fact Book, 1969*, p. 23.
[2]Securities and Exchange Commission, *Statistical Bulletin*.
[3]New York Stock Exchange, *Fact Book, 1969*, p. 16.

of corporate bonds. The data in Table 9-6 show the annual average yields of corporate Baa and Aaa bonds (Moody's series) and long-term Treasury bonds, together with the spread between the first two and between the last two of these (1955–1969). The data reveal that the three series rose and fell together, but not in the same degree. The differential between Aaa and Baa bond yields and between Aaa corporate and long-term Treasury bond yields was by no means uniform through time, reflecting the differences in demand for and supply of securities of different quality.

As yields in general rise, the premium for risk and poorer liquidity tends to increase, although this relationship has been by no means uniform. In years of recession, such as 1958, 1960, and 1961, investors require higher compensation for lesser quality, as indicated by the larger spreads among the Treasury, Aaa, and Baa groups. In 1962 through 1964, declining spreads reflected an opposite tendency. In years of sharply rising interest rates, such as 1966 through 1969, the lower quality bonds suffer most from the credit squeeze, and the spreads widen. When the market yields on both Treasury bonds and corporate bonds reached record heights in 1966 through 1969, corporates were obliged to offer yields that had not been seen in the United States for over 100 years. In September 1969, Aaa-grade corporate bonds (Moody's series) yielded an astronomical 7.3 per cent. A new offering of Cincinnati & Suburban Bell Telephone Company (rated Aaa) brought 8.25 per cent. An A-rated issue of Household Finance Corporation debentures brought 8.8 per cent—the highest yield in history on bonds of this quality.

Table 9-6.   Yields on Corporate and Treasury Bonds, 1955–1969

| | Corporate | | | U.S. Treasury | |
	Baa (1)	Aaa (2)	Spread (1) over (2)	Long Term (3)	Spread (2) over (3)
1955	3.53	3.06	0.47	2.84	0.22
1956	3.88	3.36	0.52	3.08	0.28
1957	4.71	3.89	0.82	3.47	0.42
1958	4.73	3.79	0.94	3.43	0.36
1959	5.05	4.38	0.67	4.07	0.31
1960	5.19	4.41	0.78	4.01	0.40
1961	5.08	4.35	0.73	3.90	0.45
1962	5.02	4.33	0.69	3.95	0.38
1963	4.86	4.26	0.60	4.00	0.26
1964	4.83	4.40	0.43	4.15	0.25
1965	4.87	4.49	0.38	4.21	0.28
1966	5.67	5.13	0.44	4.65	0.48
1967	6.23	5.51	0.72	4.85	0.66
1968	6.94	6.18	0.76	5.26	0.92
1969*	7.73	6.97	0.76	6.05	0.92

*Eleven months.

```
101010101010101010101010101010101010101010101010101010101010101010101010101010
101010101010101010101010101010101010101010101010101010101010101010101010101010
101010101010101010101010101010101010101   10101   101010101010101010101010101010
101010101010101010101010101010101010101010   010   0101010101010101010101010101010
101010101010101010101010101010101010101   1   101010101010101010101010101010
101010101010101010101010101010101010101010   0101010101010101010101010101010
101010101010101010101010101010101010101010101   101010101010101010101010101010
101010101010101010101010101010101010101010   0101010101010101010101010101010
101010101010101010101010101010101010101   1   101010101010101010101010101010
101010101010101010101010101010101010101010   010   0101010101010101010101010101010
101010101010101010101010101010101010101   10101   101010101010101010101010101010
101010101010101010101010101010101010101010101010101010101010101010101010101010
101010101010101010101010101010101010101010101010101010101010101010101010101010
```

The Corporate Stock Market

Definitions and Concepts

No attempt is made in this book to describe all the legal and financial characteristics of stocks or their role in corporate financial policy. Our concern is with the nature and scope of their primary and secondary markets. A few reminders of their basic features are, however, appropriate.

Corporate stock in the form of transferable certificates represents the equity interest in the company. Each share constitutes a percentage of the total net worth. The owners of the certificates enjoy the basic rights of proprietorship, some of which are, however, delegated to directors and officers or are limited by the corporate charter.

As the residual equity in the company, common stock participates in net assets in liquidation and in net earnings (when declared in dividends) after all claims of creditors and the preferences of any preferred stock have been met. The net assets and earnings, and so the prices of common stocks, are volatile, but the possibility of very high earnings gives these instruments unusual investment and speculative appeal. Their quality ranges from worthless to very high.

Preferred stock ranks above the common in preference to assets and dividends. Participation in assets in liquidation is limited to par or a stated preference value; dividends are usually set in the charter at a maximum rate that must be paid before any dividends go to the common. Such dividends are ordinarily cumulative, that is, all past preferred dividends must be paid before any can be paid to the common. Because of their preferences and limitations, preferred stocks possess some of the attributes of bonds. Indeed, the very strongest preferreds rival bonds in strength and yield. Weak preferreds are akin to common stocks in that their dividend prospects are contingent on uncertain earnings and dividends.

Convertible preferred stocks have a dual appeal. They offer the owner the option of exchange into common stock at a predetermined ratio, and so their prices and yields reflect the prospects of the common itself. The conversion feature has little or no value if the market value of the preferred is well above that of the common shares into which it is convertible. The preferred then sells at its "straight" value. When the market price of the common approaches or exceeds the conversion price, the value of the preferred equals (or exceeds) that of the number of shares of common for which it may be exchanged. This appeal applies to convertible bonds also.

The market value of common stock is mainly a function of its prospective earnings and dividends. Its asset (book) value may have some influence, as will its marketability, that is, access to a good volume of trading. The price-earnings multiplier reflects opinion on the future stability and growth of earnings and dividends. The dividend yields of common stocks are a function of their present and estimated future dividend rates.

Neither common nor preferred stock has a maturity date. Principal can ordinarily be recovered only through resale. However, two standard provisions of preferred stock give it some of the maturity features of bonds: (1) the right of the issuer to call in the stock at a value set by the charter—the call price forms a plateau or peg through which the market price is unlikely to break unless the stock is convertible or unless call is very unlikely; (2) many preferreds, especially of industrial companies, have a sinking fund or repurchase clause that requires the issuer regularly to retire shares at either a fixed rate or one contingent on earnings. Steady retirement for sinking fund has a supporting influence on market price.

Outstanding Corporate Stock

The precise market value of all publicly held corporate stocks is unknown because accurate data are unavailable on thousands of small unlisted issues. The annual year-end data from 1960 to 1968 in Table 10-1 are derived by deducting from the Federal Reserve flow-of-funds figures of the value of all corporate stock (less investment company shares) the value of listed stock as reported by the Securities and

**Table 10-1.   Estimated Value of Corporate Stocks,
1960–1968, Billions of Dollars**

	1960	1961	1962	1963	1964	1965	1966	1967	1968*
Value of all stocks	$434	$551	$484	$571	$655	$743	$666	$822	$980
Value of listed stocks	335	426	374	442	507	573	514	653	780
Value of active unlisted stocks	69	105	90	99	111	130	109	128	150
Value of inactive unlisted stocks	30	20	20	30	37	40	33	41	50

*Estimated.
Sources: *Federal Reserve Bulletin*, flow-of-funds tables; Securities and Exchange Commission, *Annual Reports*.

Exchange Commission and an estimate of active unlisted stocks. The balance represents securities of small and closely held companies. The data reveal both the volatility and the secular rise in common stock values. The chief factor causing the long-term growth has been appreciation in price rather than increases in the number of issues traded.

The Primary Market for New Stock Issues

New corporate stocks are sold to investors both directly by the issuers and indirectly through investment bankers and dealers. Direct selling is employed by new, weak, and speculative concerns that cannot obtain or afford the services of an investment banker. Sale of securities to employees and executives in connection with savings, stock purchase, and stock option incentives is also direct. Few stock issues are privately placed with institutional buyers; these are chiefly higher-grade preferred stocks of public utility companies.

The chief means of direct sale of common stocks is through the issuance of rights to existing stockholders entitling them to buy new shares (and convertible bonds and preferred) in proportion to existing holdings. Such "privileged subscriptions" are offered at a discount from current market price; the value of the right itself is determined by the difference between market and subscription price, adjusted for the increase in the number of shares. In some states, the "preemptive right" is required, in others it is optional; and in the latter states the corporate charter may require it. Where optional, management assesses the advantages of this method of financing in comparison with either public offering of stock or some other means of financing.

Successful sale of common stock (and of convertible bonds and preferred) through rights is easiest when the existing stock is already widely held and traded, when the stockholders are enthusiastic and wish to add to their holdings, when the general stock market outlook is favorable, and when the discount below market price is substantial.

The investment banker often participates in the offering of stock through rights by entering into a standby agreement by which, for a fee, he (or a syndicate) agrees to take up any shares not subscribed by stockholders.

A rough approximation of the amount of securities sold by privileged subscription, for the 12 months ending June 30, 1968, regardless of whether the sale was accompanied by standby underwriting, is indicated by the size of the "to security holders" figure (Table 10-2) within the total of securities offered for immediate cash sale and registered with the Securities and Exchange Commission. The data exclude private placements, categories such as railroad securities that need not be registered, and exempt small issues. About 7 per cent of the bond and preferred stock total was sold directly to security holders, reflecting the importance of financing with convertible issues. These are usually sold through rights to common stockholders so that the latter may retain their proportions of outstanding and potential shares. About one quarter of the new common stock was offered through privileged subscription. This low ratio is explained by the large amount of financing done by new companies and by those "going public" during this time.

Table 10-2.   Registered Securities Offered for Cash Sale, Year Ended June 30, 1968, Millions of Dollars

	Bonds	Preferred	Common	Total
To the general public	$11,899	$596	$2,088	$14,583
To security holders	686	301	729	1,716
To others	18	9	37	64
Total	$12,603	$906	$2,854	$16,363

Source: Securities and Exchange Commission, *34th Annual Report* (1968), p. 178.

Where stock is sold to the public, the use of investment bankers and syndicates depends on the size and quality of the issue and on the range of services needed by the·issuers and for which they are willing to pay.

It is convenient at this point to summarize the various methods of sale of new bond and stock issues:

(1) Direct sale without investment banker assistance:
    (a)   Small, new, and weaker issues (bonds and stocks)
    (b)   Employee and executive purchase (stocks)
    (c)   Privileged subscriptions without standby underwriting (convertible bonds and preferred stock, common stock)
(2) Direct sale with some investment banking services:
    (a)   Privileged subscriptions with standby underwriting
    (b)   Private sale to institutions, the banker acting as finder (bonds, preferred stock)
(3) Sale through investment bankers:
    (a)   On an agency or best-efforts basis (mainly stocks)
    (b)   Full commitment underwriting (all types of securities)

Table 10-3.   Methods of Distribution, Registered Securities Offered for
Cash Sale, Year Ended June 30, 1968, Millions of Dollars

	Bonds	Preferred Stock	Common Stock	Total
Underwritten (standby and full)	$12,485	$881	$1,949	$15,315
Agency sale	11	1	210	222
Direct sale	107	24	695	826
Total	$12,603	$906	$2,854	$16,363

Source: Securities and Exchange Commission, *Statistical Bulletin.*

The relative importance of the above methods is indicated by the
data in Table 10-3 on all new cash sales of securities (bonds and stocks)
that were registered with the Securities and Exchange Commission in
the year ending June 30, 1968.

Volume and Buyers of New Common Stock Issues

The changing use of common and preferred stock in business financing and their importance relative to bonds are indicated by the data
in Table 10-4 covering the gross proceeds of all new corporate securities
sold for cash in the United States for both new money and refinancing,
1960 through 1968. The figures include all public and private sales and
all registered or unregistered issues.

The volume of bond financing has been much less volatile than that
of common stocks; in 1965 through 1967, it rose sharply, reflecting the
need of funds for corporate expansion and the weakness in common
stock prices. But a major influence in 1967 and 1968 on the volume
of both bonds and preferred stocks was the fact that about 20 per cent of
the total volume consisted of convertible issues. These have their greatest appeal when stock markets are rising. Their issuance has expanded
also because of their usefulness in merger financing. Convertibles continued to be important in 1968, but the general decline in bond and
preferred stock financing reflected the high interest rates that pre-

Table 10-4.   Types of New Securities Sold for Cash,
1960–1968, Billions of Dollars

	1960	1961	1962	1963	1964	1965	1966	1967	1968
Bonds, notes, and debentures	$ 8.1	$ 9.4	$ 9.0	$10.9	$10.9	$13.7	$15.6	$22.0	$17.4
Preferred stock	0.4	0.4	0.4	0.3	0.4	0.7	0.6	0.9	0.6
Common stock	1.7	3.3	1.3	1.0	2.7	1.5	1.9	1.9	3.9
Total	$10.2	$13.1	$10.8	$12.2	$14.0	$16.0	$18.1	$24.8	$21.9

Sources: Securities and Exchange Commission, *Annual Reports* and *Statistical Bulletin.*

vailed, together with the sharp emphasis on common stock financing. Sale of preferred stock has continued to provide a relatively small amount of funds. Preferred stock lacks the tax advantage of bonds to the issuer and, with the exception of convertibles, the appreciation possibilities of common stock to the investor. The chief market for high-grade preferred stocks lies with taxed institutions that are seeking income and that enjoy the exemption of 85 per cent of dividends from Federal income taxes.

Common stock financing rose sharply in 1961, encouraged by general prosperity and rising stock prices. The decline in 1962 and 1963 is attributable to the sharp fall in stock prices (about 25 per cent) in the former year and the reluctance of companies to finance with common stock in 1963 in spite of market recovery and general prosperity. Also, financing from internal sources continued to enjoy a strong preference (see p. 113).

By 1964, common stock financing had regained favor, but weakness reappeared in 1966 and 1967 because of the sharp market decline in 1966 that maintained its impact in the following year. In 1968, with a strong market, high interest rates on bonds, and general corporate expansion, common stock financing reached its highest peak in the postwar period as both old and new companies sought equity capital in a favorable market. In the first half of 1969, in spite of a weak market, the rate of new common stock financing actually increased compared with the previous year.

Data in the previous chapter show that the major sources of corporate funds have been internal—retained profits and depreciation allowances. The small volume of new common stock financing save for years like 1964 and 1968 suggests the minor importance of the primary stock market as a source. No new railroad common stocks have been offered for cash for 40 years. Manufacturing, public utility, financial, and real estate companies have been the chief suppliers of new common stocks; they sold 60 per cent of all new common stock sold publicly in 1968.

Not all stock issues provide additional corporate funds. A large share of new issues refinances existing securities. A substantial amount —as in 1961 and 1968—represents a mere transfer of ownership of existing companies "going public" for the first time.

The growing importance of an institutional market for new stock issues is revealed by the data in Table 10-5, which combine the figures presented in the institutional chapters and attribute the balance to foreign investors and individuals. To avoid double-counting, the figures exclude issues of investment companies. The "individuals and others" group includes bank-administered trust funds, foundations and other nonprofit organizations, and minor institutions. The data represent only the net increases in stock outstanding after deducting issues sold for refinancing and those retired from earnings. Hence they

Table 10-5.   Annual Net Acquisitions of Corporate Stock,
1960–1968, Billions of Dollars

	1960	1961	1962	1963	1964	1965	1966	1967	1968
Mutual savings banks	$ —	$0.1	$0.2	$0.1	$0.1	$0.1	$0.1	$0.2	$0.2
Life insurance companies	0.4	0.4	0.4	0.2	0.4	0.7	0.3	1.0	1.2*
Property and liability insurance companies	0.1	0.3	0.4	0.5	0.3	—0.1	0.1	0.9	1.0*
Corporate pension funds	1.9	2.2	2.2	2.2	2.3	3.1	3.7	5.2	5.8
State and local government retirement funds	0.1	0.1	0.2	0.2	0.3	0.3	0.5	0.6	0.9
Investment companies (mutual)	0.8	1.1	1.0	0.7	0.8	1.2	1.0	1.4	1.2
Foreign investors	0.2	0.3	0.1	0.2	0.3	—0.4	—0.3	0.8	2.3*
Individuals and others	—1.7	—1.8	—3.7	—4.2	—3.1	—4.8	—4.2	—7.8	—13.5*
Total	$1.7	$2.7	$0.7	$—0.2	$1.4	$ —	$1.2	$2.3	$—0.9*

*Estimated.
Sources: Securities and Exchange Commission, *Annual Reports* and *Statistical Bulletin;* Bankers Trust Company, *The Investment Outlook* (annual). See also references, Chapters 3–6. Certain columns do not add to totals because of rounding.

do not show the full activity of the various institutions in the primary market for stocks.

The fact that in 1960 through 1968 institutional holdings of stocks grew more than the net increase in total outstanding stocks means that most of their acquisitions were in the open market. The individuals and others category acquired most of the new issues, but were net sellers on balance. Institutions, such as pension funds and investment companies, absorbed more than all the new financing. This increased holding provided very important support to the market for stocks, both new and old and especially the higher-grade stocks, and contributed to a shift in ownership of the better stocks into institutional hands. However, the "individuals and others" category includes bank-administered trust funds and charitable and other foundations. The extent of the sell-off by individuals per se is unknown in exact terms.

The minus figures for total new stock acquisitions in 1963 and 1968 show that in those years corporations as a whole retired more stock for treasury than they issued. The dollar amount of stock outstanding actually declined. This decline again points up the fact that companies increasingly rely on internal sources of funds rather than on new stock financing, although new stock financing did rebound in 1968.

The most noticeable shift revealed by the data is the substantial reduction in the holdings of individuals, bank trustees, and minor institutions that characterized the whole period. As a group, these investors were net sellers of stock. Especially dramatic were the reductions in 1967 and 1968. The increasing accumulations of major institutions were the chief offsetting factor. Such a shift had very important implications for the stock market (see p. 132).

Organization of the Secondary Market for Stocks

Securities markets aid in the mobilization of capital and in the transfer of savings by providing facilities for orderly trading. On the organized exchanges, listed securities are bought and sold on an auction basis through brokers. On the over-the-counter market, prices are determined mainly by negotiations between buyers and sellers through dealers acting as principals.

The organized exchanges provide a continuous market for the exchange of outstanding issues that meet the listing requirements. But mere listing does not automatically guarantee good marketability, that is, a volume of trading large enough that trades can be made with a minimum of price movement. There are a number of relatively inactive listed stocks.

The New York Stock Exchange, which has the strictest listing requirements and serves as a prototype of the other exchanges, is a voluntary association of 1,366 members (January 1, 1969), comprising mainly partners and stockholders in 646 commission houses devoted to the handling of orders on the floor of the exchange. These members represent their member firms or corporations whose other partners or stockholders are known as allied members. As of the end of 1968, 1,767 stock issues of 1,273 different companies were listed, including 1,253 commons (including 25 foreign) and 514 preferred. The market value of the stocks listed at the end of 1968 was $692 billions, and the value of trades in stocks during 1968 was $145 billions.[1]

The American Stock Exchange (also located in New York) lists the securities of smaller and younger companies than those that qualify for the "Big Board." But its activity has increased greatly in recent years; in 1968, it handled nearly 35 per cent of the number, and 18 per cent of the market value of shares traded on all organized exchanges.

The eleven regional exchanges provide trading facilities for stocks with a local interest, but the bulk of their activity is in "Big Board" issues that are also listed on the regionals ("multiple listing").

With the great increase in share ownership, especially by institutions, arrangements for buying and selling large blocks, using the facilities of the New York Stock Exchange, have become very important. The customer who originates the block pays a commission that may run three or four times the rate for auction transactions. The important arrangements are (1) exchange distributions (or acquisitions), through which a broker accumulates orders for sale (or purchase) and then fills the order on the floor of the exchange at prices between the current

---

[1]New York Stock Exchange, *Fact Book, 1969.*

bid and asked quotations; (2) secondary distributions (used to handle very large orders), for which the exchange member usually acts as a dealer, combining with other dealers to effect the sale after trading hours at a fixed price.[2]

Far more securities are traded on the unlisted or over-the-counter market—perhaps 50,000 in all, of which about 14,000 stocks and 3,500 bonds are actively traded—than on the registered exchanges. Transactions in Federal securities are offboard, as are those of all but a few state and municipal bonds. Most corporate bonds are unlisted, as are all but a few bank, insurance, and mutual fund shares and a large number of industrial and utility shares. Over-the-counter sales (exclusive of mutual fund shares) grew from $4.9 billions, or 31 per cent of all stock sales, in 1949 to $38.9 billions, or 37 per cent, in 1961.[3] On a sample day in 1965 (August 22), over-the-counter sales amounted to 30 per cent of the number of shares and 14½ per cent of the dollar value of trading on all exchanges.[4] At the end of 1968 the value of stocks actively traded over the counter was estimated at $150 billions, about 20 per cent of the aggregate of the market value traded on organized exchanges (see p. 123).

Trading on the over-the-counter market is not confined to unlisted securities. A number of listed securities are bought and sold in the "third market," which consists of dealers with an inventory of listed stocks. Perhaps 25 per cent of all over-the-counter transactions are in securities listed on exchanges, mainly Federal bonds and corporate bonds. The volume of unlisted trading in stocks listed on the New York Stock Exchange was $5.9 billions (1968), or 3.6 per cent of the volume on the exchange.[5]

Rudiments of a "fourth market" are beginning to appear. Here the institutions interested in stocks effect direct purchases and sales among themselves, without the services of a broker or dealer. In 1969, work was being done on a computerized method of matching orders for securities that would in effect constitute a new exchange and a possible threat to the monopoly of the "Big Board" for large transactions.[6]

Active markets in which transfers can be made easily and quickly contribute substantially to economic growth. Without such facilities, capital formation is unlikely to achieve a high level. Those who own the instruments representing economic capital must be assured of a fast, fair, orderly, and open system of purchase and sale at known prices.

---

[2]In 1968, 20.3 million shares with a value of over $1 billion were offered through 85 exchange distributions, and 2.3 million shares worth $82.5 millions through secondary distributions. New York Stock Exchange, *Fact Book, 1969*, p. 15.

[3]*Report of the Special Study of Securities Markets of the Securities and Exchange Commission*, House Document No. 95, 88th Cong., 1st sess., 1963, Part 2, p. 547.

[4]*Over-the-Counter Markets Study*, prepared by Booz, Allen & Hamilton, Inc., for the National Association of Securities Dealers, Inc. (New York, August 1966).

[5]Securities and Exchange Commission, *Statistical Bulletin* (March 1969), p. 12.

[6]*Business Week*, June 14, 1969, p. 104.

This is the aim of regulation of the exchanges and of dealers and brokers by the Securities and Exchange Commission under the terms of the Securities Exchange Act.

Ownership of Corporate Stock

At the end of 1968 over 26 million individuals or 13 per cent of the United States population, owned stock of publicly held corporations, compared with about 17 millions in 1962.[7] A very large number—possibly 100 millions—have an indirect interest through investing institutions and trust funds. Such "people's capitalism" has significant implications for individual companies seeking financing and for the economy as a whole. The broadening base of share ownership provides an important potential expansion to the capital market.

Data on the distribution of all outstanding stocks, especially institutional holdings, are incomplete or inconsistent. Opinion differs concerning the value of all corporate stocks outstanding—a difficult estimate because of lack of firm information on over-the-counter stocks. The list of institutions holding stocks also differs from source to source. The Securities and Exchange Commission showed institutions holding $285 billions, or 34 per cent of total stock outstanding, at the end of 1968—an increase from $176 billions, or 24 per cent, in 1964.[8] But the figure for the value of all stock outstanding differs considerably from that calculated in the Federal Reserve flow-of-funds data (see p. 123), and the list of institutions includes bank personal trust funds, which are nominal but not actual owners of shares. The holdings of the institutions discussed in this book are totaled on p. 131.

The New York Stock Exchange regularly reports institutional holdings of shares traded on that exchange. At the end of 1968, this particular list of financial institutions held $155 billions, or 22 per cent of the market value of all Exchange listed stock.[9] Corporate and other private noninsured pension funds were the largest holders ($58 billions—an increase of $9 billions over 1967); mutual investment companies continued to hold over 5 per cent of the total. The steady buying of institutions provides powerful support to the market for better quality stocks when their policy is to keep fully invested. Their laggard participation in the market—as in 1962, 1966, and 1969—has contributed to its weakness.

The steady shift in stock ownership (as measured by dollar amount) to institutions reflects not only the growth of savings held by them,

[7]Sources: New York Stock Exchange release, January 29, 1969; New York Stock Exchange, *The 17 Million: 1962 Census of Shareholders in America* (New York, June 1962). See also E. B. Cox, *Trends in the Distribution of Stock Ownership* (Philadelphia: University of Pennsylvania Press, 1963).

[8]Securities and Exchange Commission, *Statistical Bulletin* (May 1969), p. 26.

[9]New York Stock Exchange, *Fact Book, 1969*, p. 45. See also New York Stock Exchange, *Institutional Shareownership* (New York, 1964).

but also their increasing interest in common stocks as investments in a growing and inflationary economy. The *relative* decline in individuals' holdings was accelerated by the big breaks in stock prices in 1962, 1966, and 1969. But the number of shareholders continues to increase, largely as a result of growing ownership of mutual fund shares; and the value of shares held by individuals continues to rise over the long run with the secular rise in stock prices.

Collecting the data on institutional holdings of publicly held stocks from Chapters 3–6 provides the summary of institutional ownership (at year end) and the percentages of the value of all stocks (listed and active unlisted) outstanding found in Table 10-6. Some crudity is involved because of varying methods of stock valuation, generally at market. Nevertheless, the figures do show the importance of ownership by the major institutions whose role in the capital markets we have studied. Although the totals and percentages exclude bank-administered trusts, closed-end investment companies, nonprofit corporations, and minor institutions, the increase in institutional ownership is apparent.

Stock Trading and Institutional Activity

The market value of stocks (preferred and common) traded on all registered exchanges increased from $45.2 billions in 1960 to $196.4 billions in 1968, and the number of shares traded from 1,389 millions to 5.3

Table 10-6.   Institutional Ownership of Corporate Stock, 1968, Billions of Dollars

	1955	1960	1965	1968
Mutual savings banks:				
Preferred	$ —	$ 0.3	$ 0.4	0.6
Common	0.6	0.5	1.0	1.4
Life insurance companies:				
Preferred	1.7	1.8	2.9	3.2
Common	1.9	3.2	6.2	10.0
Property and liability insurance companies:				
Preferred	0.9	0.8	1.1	1.4
Common	6.0	8.6	14.1	16.7
Corporate pension funds:				
Preferred	0.5	0.7	0.8	1.3
Common	5.1	15.8	38.9	57.9
State and local government retirement funds	0.4	0.4	1.4	4.2
Investment companies (mutual):				
Preferred	0.5	0.7	0.6	1.7
Common	6.4	14.1	30.3	44.4
Total	$ 24.0	$46.9	$ 97.7	$142.8
Market value of all active stocks*	$284.0	$404.0	$703.0	$930.0
Percentage held by above institutions	8.5	11.6	13.9	15.4

*Estimated.

billions. According to the Securities and Exchange Commission, purchases and sales of four institutional groups—private noninsured pension funds, open-end investment companies, life insurance companies,
and property-casualty companies—reached all-time record levels for the
sixth consecutive year, totaling $67 billions in 1968. This total was
equal to 34 per cent of the volume of trading on all registered
exchanges.[10] The market value of total purchases and sales by noninsured pension funds was up 22 per cent, by mutual funds up 37 per
cent, by life insurance companies up 84 per cent, and by property-
casualty companies up 77 per cent over 1967. In contrast, total exchange trading increased less than 12 per cent.

The New York Stock Exchange has measured the role played by
institutions in stock market activity for several short test periods. The
list includes all major and minor institutions; it also includes "intermediaries," or nonmember broker-dealers. The share of total exchange
volume attributed to the whole list increased from 24 per cent (September 1960) to 33 per cent (October 1966). Investment companies alone
accounted for 26 per cent in the last test period.[11]

Such figures reveal the dramatic increase in the influence of institutions on market volume and activity. And we have seen their growing
share of ownership of outstanding equities. Combining ownership of
securities and trading produces the "activity rate," or measure of turnover.[12] For major institutions this activity rate has increased steadily
in recent years, reaching 46 per cent for mutual funds alone in 1968.
This percentage means that these institutions traded nearly half of
their portfolios in that year; the rate for pension funds was 19 per cent,
life insurance companies 28 per cent, and property-casualty insurance
companies 12 per cent, in contrast to the rate for all New York Stock
Exchange stocks of 22 per cent.[13] Concern over institutional activity led
to a joint resolution of the House and Senate in 1968 which authorized
the Securities and Exchange Commission to make a thorough study of
the role and the impact of institutional investors in the stock market.
The large blocks of shares involved in many trades are of special
interest.

Stock Yields

The yields on preferred stocks in general rise and fall through time
with the general level of interest rates. The return on individual issues
reflects the estimate of the market of their quality and marketability
and any special features such as convertibility.

[10]Securities and Exchange Commission, *Statistical Bulletin* (March 1969 and May
1969). Not all trades were in listed stocks.

[11]New York Stock Exchange, *Fact Book, 1969*, pp. 47–48.

[12]The activity rate is the average of purchases and sales divided by the average
value of stock portfolio for the period.

[13]Securities and Exchange Commission, *Statistical Bulletin* (May 1969), p. 21.

The spread between the yields on high-grade preferred stocks and on high-grade or money bonds arises from the fact that the former are equity instruments. Dividends on preferred stocks are a distribution of profits and are contingent on earnings and on declaration. On issues of lower quality the spread includes a premium for additional risk.

The difference between the yields on high-grade bonds and preferred stocks has narrowed through the years, and has, in fact, been negative since 1963, as indicated by the data in Table 10-7. This difference reflects the shortage of new preferred issues, the increase in earnings of the issuers, and, most important, the special demand by institutional investors subject to income taxation who enjoy an exemption of 85 per cent of the dividend, so that, other things being equal, the dividend on preferred is worth more than the same interest on a taxable bond. Some high-grade preferred stocks have yields lower than the yields on the bonds of the same companies.

The data in Table 10-7 show the annual averages of monthly yields on Moody's Aaa industrial bond series, high-grade low-dividend industrial preferred stocks, and 125 industrial common stocks for 1950, 1955, and 1960 through 1969. Being averages, the figures do not show the annual highs and lows or change within the years selected, but they do show the diminishing premium or spread between industrial bond yields and preferred and common stock yields through the years.

Traditionally the yields on any representative group of common stocks were always substantially higher than bond yields. Their steady decline in recent years has resulted in a negative spread since 1959. The explanation lies in all the factors causing the high and increasing level of common stock prices during this period: the pressure of institutional

Table 10-7. Yields on High-Grade Bonds, Preferred Stocks, and Common Stocks, 1950–1969

	Aaa Industrial Bonds (1)	10 High-Grade Industrial Preferreds (2)	125 Industrial Common Stocks (3)	Spread (2) over (1)	Spread (3) over (1)
1950	2.55	3.52	6.51	0.97	3.96
1955	3.00	3.69	3.93	0.69	0.93
1960	4.28	4.48	3.48	0.20	−0.80
1961	4.21	4.36	3.04	0.15	−1.17
1962	4.18	4.21	3.39	0.03	−0.79
1963	4.14	4.04	3.20	−0.10	−0.94
1964	4.32	4.05	2.98	−0.32	−1.34
1965	4.45	4.07	2.98	−0.38	−1.47
1966	5.12	4.67	3.44	−0.45	−1.68
1967	5.49	5.13	3.11	−0.36	−2.38
1968	6.12	5.62	2.93	−0.51	−3.19
1969*	7.15	6.12	3.11	−1.03	−4.04

*Eleven months.
Sources: *Moody's Bond Survey, Stock Survey,* and *Moody's Industrials.*

buying, the scarcity of new stock issues in relation to the growth of corporate assets, economic prosperity and the rise in corporate profits, the fear of inflation, the tax structure and its encouragement to capital gains, and other factors too numerous to discuss here. The sharp increase in the negative spread in 1966 through 1969 reflects also the record high yields on bonds reached in those years. The negative spread will likely persist, though not in the same magnitude.

The Mortgage Market

Basic Characteristics

A mortgage is a lien on real property to secure a loan. The mortgage and the actual note are different instruments, but we shall use the term *mortgage* to represent the combination. Corporate bonds secured by pledge of fixed assets and chattel mortgages secured by personal property and business equipment are excluded from our discussion. Some secured business loans are included in the commercial mortgage category. Mortgages are almost exclusively capital-market instruments in that their ultimate maturity may run 5 to 40 years and their proceeds are used to finance mainly capital assets.

Mortgages appeal to investors because the tangible assets pledged can be inspected and valued and are property of substantial importance to the borrower. Furthermore, yields on mortgages are consistently higher than those on other fixed-income securities. The differentials reflect their specialized nature, their lesser marketability compared with that of bonds and stocks, and the delays involved in foreclosure and final settlement in the event of failure.

Most modern mortgages require the borrower to amortize the principal by remitting a periodic sum covering principal, interest, and sometimes property taxes and insurance. Early impetus to the use of amortized loans stemmed from their adoption by the Home Owners'

Loan Corporation and by savings and loan associations after the short-comings of single-principal-payment loans became apparent in the depression of the 1930's. Amortization was also required by the Federal Housing Administration for insured loans (1934) and by the Veterans Administration for guaranteed loans (1944).

Other characteristics of the modern mortgage are lower down payments, higher loan-to-value ratios, and lengthening of final maturity to as long as 40 years on some liens. Periodic repayment (often monthly) provides a turnover of investors' funds and a steady growth in the owner's equity, reducing some of the risk from this combination of features. The modern mortgage has had a tremendous impact on the real estate market, especially on home ownership, and has been at least partly responsible for the diversion of a flood of savings into real estate financing through the expansion of institutions investing in such credits.

Size and Growth

Table 1-2 shows that of all debt instruments, mortgages have had the greatest expansion in the postwar period. The net annual increase in amount outstanding—the flow of funds into mortgages—has averaged $18 billions for the period and in 1969 was running at about $27 billions a year. With $397 billions outstanding at the end of 1968, the fact that a substantial portion (possibly 10 per cent) of mortgage debt is retired each year means that the amount of new mortgage debt written each year is close to $75 billions.

Table 11-1 shows the mortgage debt outstanding at the end of se-

Table 11-1. Mortgage Debt Outstanding, at Year End, 1950–1968, Billions of Dollars

	1950	1955	1960	1965	1968*
Farm	$ 6.1	$ 9.1	$ 12.8	$ 21.2	$ 27.5
Residential:					
1–4-family	45.2	88.3	141.3	212.9	251.2
Multifamily	8.4	12.4	19.0	37.2	47.3
	$53.6	$100.7	$160.3	$250.1	$298.5
Commercial and other	13.1	20.1	33.7	54.5	71.5
Total	$72.8	$129.9	$206.8	$325.8	$397.5
Conventional and other	$50.7	$ 87.0	$144.5	$244.6	$304.7
FHA-insured	11.8	18.3	32.6	50.1	59.6
VA-guaranteed	10.3	24.6	29.7	31.1	33.2
Total	$72.8	$129.9	$206.8	$325.8	$397.5

*Preliminary.
Sources: 1950–1955: S. B. Klaman, *The Volume of Mortgage Debt in the Postwar Decade* (New York: National Bureau of Economic Research, Inc., 1958); 1960–1968: *Federal Reserve Bulletin; Housing and Home Finance Agency, Annual Reports.*

lected years in the postwar period, classified by major types of property pledged and by major types of liens.

Types

In addition to differences in size, risk, geographical origin, and other factors, mortgages can be classified in a number of ways, of which the following categories are useful for our purposes.

(1) By type of property pledged:
   Farms
   1–4-family residences
   Multifamily dwellings (apartments)
   Commercial and industrial property
(2) By level of lien:
   First mortgages
   Junior mortgages (second, third)
(3) By type of lien:
   Conventional
   Government-supported: FHA-insured, VA-guaranteed
(4) By use of property:
   Owner-occupied: residential, commercial
   Rental: Residential, commercial
(5) By type of borrower:
   Consumers
   Corporations
   Small businesses
   Farmers
(6) By purpose:
   New construction
   Acquisition of existing property
   General financing
(7) By type of lender:
   Financial institutions
   Governmental agencies
   Individuals

Farm Mortgages

Farm mortgage debt has grown somewhat less than total mortgages, and with the rise in farm property values in the postwar period the real burden has been greatly diminished. Farm debt is typically first-mortgage debt and could be described as conventional in that only a small portion is FHA- or VA-supported; it is, however, often guaranteed by other special agencies. This debt is incurred mainly for financing property, although the proceeds are sometimes used for general purposes.

As shown by Table 11-5 (p. 144), commercial banks and life insurance companies held 35 per cent of the total debt in 1968, but there has been a steady drift into the hands of governmental agencies such as the Federal Land Banks, which make long-term loans through National Farm Loan Associations (see p. 144), and the Farmers Home Administration, an agency of the Department of Agriculture, which makes 1–5 year operating loans and farm-ownership loans.[1] Individuals held about $12 billions, or 45 per cent of the total (1968). The inherent qualities of farm mortgages appeal to many local capitalists and former landowners.

Home Loans

Home mortgages have remained high in relative importance. Loans secured by 1–4-family dwellings increased from 62 per cent of debt outstanding at the end of 1950 to 63 per cent as of 1968. Their growth—now running about $15 billions a year—reflects mainly the development of home financing by savings institutions under favorable terms (see FHA and VA loans below) on an amortized basis. Population, consumer incomes, and construction costs all rose during the postwar period, as did the supply of funds available for mortgage investment. The result was a tremendous increase in home construction and financing in the early postwar period. The peak in annual private residential housing starts (1,908,000 units) was reached in 1950. Since then the figure has been as low as 1,175,000 units (1957); it suffered other declines in 1962 and 1967 when the supply of funds available for mortgages was greatly reduced or when mortgage yields were at their highs. Some recovery took place in 1968, and by the end of that year starts hit an annual rate of 1,900,000. But they fell off to a rate of 1,300,000 in the middle of 1969, which reflected the high cost of land and construction, the decline in savings available for mortgage, and the extraordinarily high interest rates required on mortgages. The chief decline was in the single-family category. The data in Table 11-2 indicate the demand for residential financing.

The three basic home mortgage loans are conventional loans without insurance or guarantee, those insured by the Federal Housing Administration, and those guaranteed by the Veterans Administration. Table 11-1 shows the amounts of each type *oustanding* at the end of selected years.

Conventional loans have consistently been the most important category, ranging around 70 per cent of the total outstanding in recent years. The annual volume of new FHA-insured loans reached its peak

---

[1]To show farm mortgage debt as separate from residential debt is not quite accurate, as the total of the former in Table 11-1 includes some mortgages incurred for home purposes.

Table 11-2. Housing Starts and Construction Costs, 1950–1968

	1950	1955	1960	1965	1968
Private nonfarm housing starts (000's)					
1-family	—	—	973	942	901
2-family and more	—	—	257	509	582
Total	1,908	1,627	1,230	1,451	1,483
Construction cost, billions of dollars	$15.6	$18.2	$16.4	$20.4	$22.4

Source: Department of Commerce, Bureau of the Census, *Construction Reports*, Series C20, C30.

in 1959. "Section 203" loans to finance new and existing dwellings are first-mortgage amortized loans bearing a maximum nominal interest rate of 8.50 per cent (1970), with the mortgagor paying an additional 0.5 per cent to the FHA mutual fund as insurance premiums. Maximum maturities range as long as 35 years, with maximum loan-value ratios as high as 97 per cent. (Other interest rates, maturities, and loan-value ratios apply to FHA-insured liens on multifamily units and other loans.)

The original fixed-interest rate on FHA home loans was 4.25 per cent. The rate was raised and lowered on several occasions, depending on its competitive position with respect to yields on conventional mortgages and on bonds. In recent years, FHA-insured liens have sold at discounts (and occasional premiums) in the secondary market to produce a satisfactory yield. But institutional investors resist their purchase at substantial discounts because of the uncertainty of their ultimate yield (many mortgages are paid off before maturity). Builders and other sellers, who have to absorb any discount—pick up the "points"— or resort to subterfuge to pass it along to the buyers, also resent the fixed nominal yield. Its elevation to 8½ per cent in late 1969 reflected the record level of interest rates then prevailing. But even this rate failed to match market yields, which were breaking through the 9 per cent level, and discounts prevailed. In the summer of 1969 a Federal Commission on Mortgage Interest Rates had recommended the abolition of fixed nominal rates for an experimental 3-year period.

Until 1961, FHA-insured loans could be purchased by qualified institutions only. Individual investors became eligible in that year, but their demand has not been substantial. The chief market is the Federal National Mortgage Association (p. 143). In 1969 the Association committed funds to their purchase at the annual rate of $8 billions.

With their controlled appraisals, stated credit standards, and amortized terms, FHA loans have had an immense effect toward standardization of lending practice. They have been chiefly responsible for the disappearance of the straight 5-year mortgage and for the acceptance of high loan-to-value ratios.

The Serviceman's Readjustment Act of 1944, as amended, provides for the guarantee by the Veterans Administration of institutional loans for the financing of veterans' homes, farms, and businesses. The maximum maturity of home loans is 30 years; the original nominal yield was 4 per cent. By 1955, such loans constituted a quarter of all home recordings of $20,000 or less. However, during 1956 through 1968, the yield rate, although frequently raised, was often unattractive relative to those on other mortgages and bonds, and VA loans sold at substantial discounts. The nominal rate was raised to 8.50 per cent late in 1969. Although VA loans with their 100 per cent loan-to-value ratio and guarantee by the Veterans Administration (to $7,500 or 60 per cent of the loan, whichever is less) are attractive, the value of new recordings and the amount outstanding have leveled out and will decline in the future as loan repayments outstrip new recordings.

Junior Mortgages

Much obscurity surrounds the amount and use of second mortgages, primarily because they are held by individuals rather than by reporting institutional investors. As of 1960, the Bureau of the Census estimated the residential dollar volume at $3.8 billions, or 2.4 per cent of residential debt outstanding.[2] The amount is probably over $9 billions today. Their revival is an interesting feature of the modern mortgage market and reflects the great postwar demand for housing that has required many buyers to present and sellers to accept a junior lien to bridge the gap between the conventional first mortgage plus available equity and the selling price of the property. Junior mortgages fill a substantial need in financing houses above the middle-income bracket that are not eligible for sufficient FHA or VA financing. This in turn stems from the restricted loan-to-value ratios required by institutional lenders.

The modern second mortgage requires rapid amortization of principal over a period seldom longer than 5 years. Steady repayment of principal, along with that of the senior mortgage, builds an increasing equity. However, subordination to the first lien requires a high yield produced by sale at a substantial discount, ranging from 8 to 15 per cent.

The seller willing to accept a second lien can retain it or, as is usually the case, sell it to a permanent holder through local mortgage brokers and dealers. Such loans are likely to be used most frequently in periods of tight money (such as in 1959, 1966, and 1969), when adequate senior financing is limited. They are also often used for general fund-raising purposes when the property already supports a first lien.

Because institutions are, in the main, prohibited from holding junior mortgages, individuals are the chief investors in such loans.

---

[2]U.S. Department of Commerce, Bureau of the Census, "Residential Finance," *Census of Housing*, V (1960), Part 2, p. xxiii.

Multifamily (Apartment) Loans

Loans secured by multifamily dwellings have run between 12 and 15 per cent of all residential loans outstanding in recent years, reflecting the rise in land values and the shift back to metropolitan living that has encouraged greater construction of apartments. Regulations governing such loans are being relaxed, and institutional investment is increasing.

The number of private nonfarm multifamily housing starts (starts other than 1-family residences) has increased substantially, rising to 582,000 in 1968. Dips in the rising secular trend occurred in 1956 and 1960, reflecting prerecession or recession conditions, and in 1965 through 1969, reflecting tight money.

Apartment loans usually have a lower loan-to-value ratio and bear lower yields than do loans on 1–4-family structures. The social presure for mass home ownership and easy financing that characterizes the single-dwelling market is lacking, except in the case of FHA-insured loans on multifamily dwellings. Each situation is considered independently through the screening process applied to rental properties in general. Large apartment loans are in demand by mutual savings banks and by life insurance companies (see Table 11-5, p. 144), and many are obtained in the national market either by direct representatives of the investors or through the efforts of local mortgage correspondents. As in the case of commercial and industrial loans, institutional investors, especially life insurance companies, have developed a preference for large mortgages on income properties and those that provide some equity participation.

Commercial and Industrial Mortgages

Loans secured by business property (other than apartments) are highly specialized instruments, mainly in amortized conventional form, with final maturities of from 10 to 30 years. They constituted 18 per cent of mortgage debt outstanding at the end of 1968. They are incurred by builders and developers for construction purposes and by business firms for general financing. Many commercial mortgages loans are classes as term loans by banks and insurance companies and are excluded from the regular mortgage category, as are mortgage bond issues.

Industrial mortgages to finance the construction and acquisition of manufacturing properties are frequently amortized in as short a period as 10 years because of their special risks. The strongest of these, as well as those based on retail shopping centers, department stores, and warehouses, are secured by property leased to large national tenants. Such mortgages are in effect two-name paper. Yields on the best of these approximate the yields on good-grade corporate bonds. Many residential construction loans that will eventually be refinanced on a permanent basis are classed as commercial until taken out by the original or ultimate investor. Thus, this category is not completely distinguishable from that of residential liens.

The Primary Mortgage Market

In Chapters 2 through 6, the role of the major institutions in supplying funds to the primary mortgage market was discussed. The demand for mortgage financing follows the housing cycle, which, in the postwar period, appears to have a longer swing than the general business cycle. When peaks and valleys do coincide either with the general cycle (as in 1957, 1958, and 1960), or with ease and tightness of capital (1966 and 1967 through 1969), marked variations appear in housing starts, construction volume, and mortgage financing. A greater variation might have taken place save for the large use of long-term Federal supported loans, which avoid the hazards of the former shorter mortgage result in much more homogeneity, and contribute to the development of a national mortgage market.

The data in Table 11-3 show the annual changes in the major categories of outstanding mortgage loans from 1960 through 1968. The

Table 11-3. Annual Changes in Mortgages, 1960–1968, Billions of Dollars

	1960	1961	1962	1963	1964	1965	1966	1967	1968
Farm	$ 0.7	$ 1.1	$ 1.3	$ 1.6	$ 2.1	$ 2.3	$ 2.1	$ 2.2	$ 2.0
1–4-family	10.4	11.8	13.4	15.7	15.4	15.3	10.7	12.5	15.4
Multifamily and commercial	4.8	6.6	7.6	8.4	8.3	8.1	8.4	8.1	9.7
Total	$16.0	$19.5	$22.3	$25.7	$25.8	$25.7	$21.2	$22.8	$27.1

Sources: *Federal Reserve Bulletin*; Federal Home Loan Bank Board. Some columns do not add to totals because of rounding.

volatility of the net flow of funds into mortgages results from variation in the amount of construction and capital-market conditions. The year 1960 was characterized by recession, and 1966 by a shortage of capital. As we saw in earlier chapters, the institutions providing the major flow of funds have varied their acquisition of mortgage investments with yields on alternative investments. Population factors and a lower level of family formation help to explain the smoothing out of 1–4-family housing starts in 1963 through 1965, and the increase in apartment demand. Tightness of capital and increasing interest rates hurt residential financing cruelly in 1966, and the volume reached former levels only in 1968. Multifamily and commercial liens greatly increased in 1968, which reflected the big rise in multifamily starts and the growing volume of commercial construction, aided by the interest of banks and other institutions in the large and higher-yielding loans.

Annual Changes in Owners' Shares

To indicate the shifts in sources of funds devoted to net new mortgage financing, the data in Table 11-4 show the annual amounts supplied by the major investors from 1960 through 1968. The investors' changing interest in various liens was discussed in earlier chapters, and so the data refer to mortgage investments as a whole.

The factors responsible for the annual flow of funds were discussed in Chapters 2 through 6. The steady increase in acquisitions by savings and loan associations was badly interrupted by the drying up of their funds in 1966; some recovery was made in 1967 and 1968, but net inflow shrank to about $2½ billions in the first 10 months of 1969. Commercial bank investment in 1968 rose above the previous high after substantial reductions in 1966 and 1967; multifamily and commercial loans accounted for much of the increase. But banks suffered a net decline in savings funds of over $10 billions in the first 10 months of 1969. Investment by savings banks shows the effect of the "credit crunch" of 1966,

Table 11-4. Annual Acquisitions of Mortgages, 1960–1968, Billions of Dollars

	1960	1961	1962	1963	1964	1965	1966	1967	1968
Commercial banks	$ 0.7	$ 1.6	$ 4.1	$ 4.9	$ 4.6	$ 5.7	$ 4.7	$ 4.6	$ 6.7
Mutual savings banks	2.0	2.2	3.2	3.9	4.3	4.1	2.7	3.0	3.0
Savings and loan associations	6.9	8.8	9.9	12.1	10.5	9.0	4.0	7.5	9.0
Life insurance companies	2.6	2.4	2.7	3.6	4.6	4.9	4.6	2.9	2.5
Corporate pension funds	0.3	0.3	0.3	0.3	0.5	0.6	0.5	0.1	0.1
State and local government retirement funds	0.3	0.5	0.2	0.4	0.4	0.7	0.8	0.6	0.4
Federal credit agencies	0.8	0.2	0.1	−1.0	0.3	0.2	2.5	1.7	2.0*
Business corporations	—	0.7	0.5	0.6	0.4	0.5	−0.6	0.4	0.6*
Individuals and others	2.4	2.8	1.3	0.9	0.2	0.1	2.0	2.8	2.8
Total	$16.0	$19.5	$22.3	$25.7	$25.8	$25.7	$21.2	$23.8	$27.1

*Estimated.
Sources: See citations in schedules, Chapters 2 through 6; Bankers Trust Company, *The Investment Outlook* (New York, annual). Some columns do not add to totals because of rounding.

and the lower rate of accumulation has continued through 1969; in general the variations have reflected the greater or lesser appeal of corporate bonds. Life insurance investment shows the volatility discussed in Chapter 4; in very recent years, high-yielding and more marketable bonds have been attractive, and in recent years home loans have lost their appeal. The role of Federal credit agencies has expanded considerably; The Federal National Mortgage Association is now the chief market for Federally supported loans. Pension fund investment increased substantially until 1967. This source may increase in the future as the fund managers become more skilled in mortgage management or rely more on servicing by mortgage correspondents. The acquisitions of individuals and minor institutions continue to show little relation to the variations in the annual net increases of total mortgages.

Ownership of Mortgages: 1968

Table 11-5 summarizes the ownership pattern of outstanding mortgage debt of all types at the end of 1968. Savings and loan associations held one-third of the total, reflecting their increasing share of single-family residential financing and their growing interest in multifamily instruments. Their preference for conventional loans is very evident. The "Individuals and others" category held 14 per cent of the total

Table 11-5.   Ownership of Mortgage Debt, December 31, 1968, Billions of Dollars

	Commercial Banks	Mutual Savings Banks	Savings and Loan Associations	Life Insurance Companies	U.S. Agencies	Individuals and Others	Total*
Farm	$ 3.7	$ 0.1	—	$ 5.8	$ 5.5†	$12.4	$ 27.5
Residential:							
1–4-family	38.8	35.0	110.3	29.6	13.2	24.3	251.2
Multifamily	2.7	11.7	10.6	12.8	1.0†	8.5	47.3
	$41.5	$46.7	$120.9	$42.4	$14.2	$32.8	$298.5
Commercial and other	20.5	6.6	9.9	21.8	—	12.7	71.5
Total	$65.7	$53.4	$130.8	$70.0	$19.7	$57.9	$397.5
Conventional and other	$55.1	$25.8	$117.1	$52.0	$ 8.3	$46.4	$304.7
FHA-insured	7.9	15.6	6.7	12.0	8.7	8.7	59.6
VA-guaranteed	2.7	12.0	7.0	6.0	2.7	2.8	33.2
Total	$65.7	$53.4	$130.8	$70.0	$19.7	$57.9	$397.5

*Preliminary.
†Estimated.
Sources: *Federal Reserve Bulletin; Journal of the Federal Home Loan Bank Board.* See also sources cited for institutions, Chapters 2 through 6.

debt, predominantly of the conventional type. They form the chief market for farm loans.

Life insurance companies are second only to savings banks in their emphasis on Federally underwritten loans. These investors use the mortgage company correspondent most heavily in the acquisition of mortgages from capital-seeking areas (see p. 148). Over one-third of the mortgage portfolios of commercial banks consisted of nonresidential loans.

If the shrinkage in net savings of institutions continues, together with the "disintermediation" or diversion of savings to open-market investments, that was evident in 1969, a shift in the ownership of mortgages will likely continue.

Mortgage Companies

We have frequently referred to the special role of mortgage companies as correspondents in originating and servicing loans for institutional investors. They deserve special emphasis in a discussion of the primary market for mortgages.

Nature and Functions

"The modern mortgage company is typically a closely held, private corporation whose principal activity is originating and servicing residential mortgage loans for institutional investors. It is subject to a minimum degree of federal or state supervision, has a comparatively small capital investment relative to its volume of business, and relies largely on commercial bank credit to finance its operations and mortgage inventory. Such inventory is usually held only for a short interim between closing mortgage loans and their delivery to ultimate investors."[3]

These firms are primarily merchants of mortgages, chiefly residential. They seek out loans, secure interim bank financing, resell the loans to institutions, and thereafter service the loans for the final owner.[4] They are not to be confused with mortgage brokers, who serve solely as intermediaries and maintain no continuous relationship with borrower or investor (see p. 149).[5]

Mortgage companies are similar to investment banking concerns

---

[3]S. B. Klaman, *The Postwar Rise of Mortgage Companies*, Occasional Paper 60 (New York: National Bureau of Economic Research, Inc., 1959), p. 1.

[4]Other activities include making construction loans, serving as mortgage dealers, and writing property insurance.

[5]Mortgage companies, as defined herein, are often known as "mortgage bankers." The latter term, however, may be appropriately applied to all institutions that engage in mortgage financing.

in that they are involved mainly in the distribution of new instruments. They originate mortgages and collect an origination fee of from 1 to 2.5 per cent from borrowers or, as is often the case for conventional loans, from the investor in the form of a premium of about 0.5 per cent above par. However, in contrast to the investment banking firm, the mortgage company operates primarily on the basis of prior and continuing relationships with the institutions it serves as "correspondent." Typically, it derives at least one-half of its income from the administration or servicing fee charged for collecting and remitting interest and principal of monthly amortized loans and from otherwise representing the investor throughout the life of the mortgage. Other income is derived from interest on mortgages held in inventory and from insurance and other ancilliary activities.[6]

By originating mortgage loans in areas needing financing and by placing them with institutions in areas enjoying surplus funds, the mortgage company has been very instrumental in the development of a national mortgage market. Its contribution was greatly accelerated by the advent of FHA-insured and VA-guaranteed loans in 1934 and 1944, respectively.

> These federal programs, providing for the underwriting of mortgages on very liberal terms to borrowers, were basic to the accelerated postwar demand for home mortgage loans, to the flow of funds from institutional investors across state borders, and to the growth of large-scale home builders and mass merchandising programs.[7]

Mortgage companies are in all states, with a concentration in the South and West, where local funds are insufficient to meet the demand for mortgage loans. The correspondent system brings in funds from the eastern capital market.

Size and Volume of Services

S. B. Klaman estimated that in 1955 there were 865 mortgage companies with combined assets of $1.8 billions and with average assets of $2.1 millions.[8] By 1968, the number had grown to well over 1,200.

---

[6]The traditional annual servicing fee has been 0.5 per cent of the outstanding principal balance of small residential loans, although lower rates have appeared recently. Fees on apartment and commercial property loans are considerably smaller because these are easier to service.

[7]Klaman, *Postwar Rise*, p. 5.

[8]Klaman, *Postwar Rise*, p. 19. As of December 31, 1968, 242 companies, representing 40 per cent of the mortgage company members of the association, had assets totaling $2.4 billions. Mortgage Bankers Association of America, *Mortgage Banking 1968: Trends, Financial Statements and Operating Ratios*, Research Committee Trends Report No. 7 (Washington, 1969), Table 6a.

Assets and net worth are not, however, the best measures of operations because outside funds, chiefly bank loans, support mortgages held in inventory. The volume of mortgages serviced is the best indicator.[9] The 804 correspondent company members (1968) of the Mortgage Bankers Association of America serviced $69 billions of mortgages in 1968, or 17 per cent of the outstanding total. Their emphasis was on loans on 1–family properties, of which they serviced $53 billions, or 21 per cent of the total.[10] Thirty-six per cent of the companies are currently servicing a volume of less than $20 millions; at the other extreme, 178 companies service a volume of $100 millions or more, and at least 30 companies a volume of $400 millions or more.[11]

Sources of Funds

Bank loans are used to carry two types of mortgages those for which investors have made advance commitments but which will be delivered later and those accumulated for later placement when the opportunity arises. An extensive "warehousing" operation requires a sufficient spread between the rate on bank loans and the mortgage rates. The operations of the mortgage company are therefore directly affected by changes in general credit policy.

At the end of 1968, a sample of 242 of the 804 mortgage company members of the Mortgage Bankers Association of America showed bank notes payable of 72 per cent of total assets, compared with 13 per cent representing net worth.[12]

Uses of Funds

In 1968, for all mortgage companies combined, it was estimated that mortgage loan inventory constituted 57 per cent and construction loans 22 per cent of total assets.[13] It is not surprising that FHA-insured and VA-guaranteed loans on 1–4-family houses predominated. The FHA mortgage (and later the VA-guaranteed mortgage) avoided state restrictions on loan-to-value ratios, overcame the diverse foreclosure requirements in the various states, and with its uniform property requirements and appraised procedures became "outwardly a negotiable

---

[9] As Colean points out, "a company that made loans only on commitment from an investing institution would show less assets than one that inventoried loans by the use of bank credit for uncommitted future sale, even though the volume of business done might be the same in both cases." M. L. Colean, *Mortgage Companies: Their Place in the Financial Structure*, a monograph prepared for the Commission on Money and Credit (Englewood Cliffs, N.J.: Prentice-Hall, Inc., 1962), p. 8.

[10] Mortgage Bankers Association of America, *Mortgage Banking.*

[11] Mortgage Bankers Association of America, *Mortgage Banking.*

[12] Mortgage Bankers Association of America, *Mortgage Banking.*

[13] Mortgage Bankers Association of America, *Mortgage Banking.*

instrument of general acceptability."[14] The conditions making for the development of a national market led to a broad geographical distribution in which the mortgage company played the leading role. At the end of 1968, mortgage companies were servicing $51 billions of Federally underwritten mortgages, or 55 per cent of the total outstanding.[15]

Role in the Mortgage Market

Mortgage companies perform their role of originators and servicers of mortgages through their relationships with three institutional investors. In 1968, 45 per cent of their servicing volume was for life insurance companies; 22 per cent, for mutual savings banks; and 12 per cent, for the Federal National Mortgage Association.[16] They do relatively little business with savings and loan associations, which typically originate and service their own credits, and service a modest amount for commercial banks. Mortgage companies are also the principal users of the FNMA as a secondary market.

In 1968 and 1969 mortgage companies lost much of their traditional role of originators of home mortgages as institutions diverted funds to other investments. Mortgage companies had to develop more loans on income properties and offer incentives such as variable yields, equity participations and other "kickers" to attract funds, especially from life insurance companies.

Large institutional investors are originating more of their own loans than before, and commercial banks are entering the servicing field, so that mortgage companies are broadening their activities to include holding more permanent inventories of mortgages, selling more to individual investors and to pension funds, and expanding related lines of business such as real estate brokerage and insurance. Such an expanded role will require further growth in the size and resources of the typical company.

The Secondary Mortgage Market

Three basic transactions take place in the total mortgage market: (1) origination and holding of mortgages by investors; (2) origination of mortgages by investors and mortgage companies as agents with prior commitments to deliver them to other investors, who are in effect the principals—here the ultimate investor makes the investment decisions and takes the risks; (3) transfer of outstanding mortgages from old owners to new. Secondary market activity involves the third operation.

The secondary market was primarily local in scope until the advent

---

[14]Colean, *Mortgage Companies*, p. 23.
[15]Mortgage Bankers Association of America, *Mortgage Banking.*
[16]Mortgage Bankers Association of America, *Mortgage Banking.*

of FHA-insured and VA-guaranteed loans in 1934 and 1944, respectively. As we have seen, the uniformity of standards and terms and the new feature of government support gave these instruments homogeneity, and thus made them readily transferable, and facilitated the flow of mortgage funds across geographical barriers. In recent years, conventional loans have been taking on common characteristics, but each one still represents a separate credit risk.[17]

Individual and institutional investors use the secondary market to acquire and sell mortgages—chiefly residential—either directly through their own contacts or through mortgage brokers.[18] Most of the latter are local concerns, although a few large firms in big cities operate on a national scale. Investors sell mortgages through brokers to switch funds into other assets or to acquire them for immediate delivery to round out portfolio requirements that have not been fulfilled by advance commitments. The brokers' commissions on secondary transfers run from 0.25 per cent to 0.5 per cent, depending mainly on the size of the loan.

Commercial banks make construction loans for later retention or resale. They "warehouse" loans as inventory that can be liquidated or held and transact transfers among families. Savings banks seldom use the secondary market. Insurance companies do not make construction loans but acquire permanent loans from others and resell a very modest amount. Savings and loan associations originate virtually all their mortgage holdings but do some construction financing that may be transferred to others and occasionally turn to the secondary market for portfolio needs. As we have seen, mortgage companies are engaged mainly in originating loans for resale to others. Their activities in the secondary market are modest. Individuals and Federal agencies deal primarily in the secondary market. The special secondary market through the FNMA deserves separate discussion.

Federal National Mortgage Association

The original purpose of the FNMA in 1938 was to provide a secondary market for Federally supported residential mortgages. This goal has been realized to only a limited extent. From 1938 to 1948, its activity was confined to modest transactions in FHA mortgages to help equalize the flow of funds for mortgage investment and the demand for financing.

---

[17]In recent years, about a dozen privately owned companies have been established to insure conventional mortgages. Examples are Continental Mortgage Insurance, Inc., and Mortgage Guarantee Insurance Corporation. The latter accounts for about 75 per cent of private insurance written (over $3 billions of insurance in force at the end of 1966). *Savings and Loan News* (March 1968), p. 56.

[18]These should not be confused with mortgage banking companies as described previously.

In 1948, the Association was rechartered. Its chief function, however, was to serve as a primary source of funds by acquiring FHA, VA, and Federal housing mortgages through mortgage companies and institutions acting as originating agents. Prices were to be supported by buying loans at par and holding them to maturity. In 1954, the basic functions were redefined; (1) management and liquidation of mortgages acquired from a variety of other government agencies, (2) special assistance programs for subsidized housing and other government home programs, and (3) secondary market operations in which FHA and VA mortgages were to be acquired from mortgage companies and institutions. The first two activities were financed by borrowing from the Treasury and by selling participation certificates secured by mortgages in portfolio. The third activity has been financed through the sale of debentures and discount notes, loans from the Treasury, and issuance of stock—common stock to member associations and individuals and preferred stock to the Treasury.

Under its secondary market operations, FNMA bought and sold FHA and VA mortgages at premiums or discounts that reflected the difference between their fixed nominal rates and the required market rates. Activity increased greatly in the 1960's; purchases reached a peak of $2.1 billions in 1966 to relieve the tight money situation of that year. Purchases declined in 1967 and 1968 but reached $1.9 billions in 1968. Very few sales were made during the middle and later 1960's.

In September 1968, under Title VIII of the Housing and Urban Redevelopment Act, the management and liquidation and the special assistance functions were transferred to a new agency, the Government National Mortgage Association (GNMA). After the retirement of its preferred stock, FNMA became a separate and private corporation. Its secondary market operations, under which purchases had been determined by the volume of government-supported mortgages attracted at market yields, were shifted to a "free market" system. FNMA now deals in commitments rather than in mortgages. Each week the Association indicates the total volume of forward commitments it will make to purchase eligible mortgages within 3 months, 6 months, and 1 year, leaving prices (and yields) to be determined by bidders at auction. In the autumn of 1969, FNMA held $9.8 billions, and GNMA, $4.7 billions of FHA and VA mortgages, together holding 15 per cent of these instruments outstanding.[19]

FNMA has contributed significantly to the development of a secondary market. The new GNMA has the authority to guarantee the principal and interest of securities backed by FHA and VA mortgages and issued by FNMA or other approved agencies. So some progress is being made in so far as a market for government-supported liens is concerned. But there are still obstacles to the free flow of mortgage

---

[19]*Federal Reserve Bulletin.*

money to and from individuals and institutions on a national scale, and geographical differences in yields still appear. As for conventional loans, institutions have been going outside their local territories in greater amount than before, and the activity of mortgage bankers has aided in attracting funds (when surplus funds exist) to capital-starved areas. But a national market is still rudimentary.

Mortgage Yields

The data in Table 11-6 provide mortgage-yield information from 1955 through 1969; the figures compare the national averages of conventional and FHA mortgages and the yields on conventionals in the West. The crudities of geographical and annual averages should not be overlooked. The data reveal the variations in mortgage yields as conditions in the capital market have changed. Tight money conditions in 1957, 1959, 1960, and 1966 through 1969 show up in all the mortgage series and in the bond rate. Yields on FHA mortgages (for purchases of new homes) were less variable than those on conventionals because of standardization and the influence of the fixed nominal rate. The first column reveals that this latter rate was reduced in only one year (1961). Comparison of the first two columns reveals that, using annual averages, FHA mortgages have sold at a discount in the secondary market. Their average yield in November 1969 was 8.5 per cent. Conventional yields to finance new homes were consistently above

Table 11-6. Yields on Mortgages and Bonds, 1955–1969

| | FHA Mortgages (Sec. 203) | | Conventional Home Mortgages | | Aaa Corporate Bonds, Per Cent |
	Contract Rate, Per Cent	Market Yield, Per Cent	National Average, Per Cent	Western Average, Per Cent	
1955	4.5	4.6	5.2	5.4	3.06
1956	4.5–5.0	4.8	5.4	5.5	3.36
1957	5.0–5.25	5.4	5.8	6.1	3.89
1958	5.25	5.5	5.7	6.1	3.79
1959	5.25–5.75	5.7	6.0	6.4	4.38
1960	5.75	6.2	6.2	6.7	4.41
1961	5.75–5.25	5.8	6.0	6.5	4.35
1962	5.25	5.6	5.9	6.3	4.33
1963	5.25	5.5	5.9	6.4	4.26
1964	5.25	5.5	5.8	6.3	4.40
1965	5.25	5.5	5.8	6.4	4.49
1966	5.25–6.00	6.4	6.4	6.5	5.13
1967	6.00	6.6	6.3	6.6	5.51
1968	6.00–6.75	7.1	6.8	6.9	6.18
1969*	6.75–8.50	8.0	7.6	8.1	6.97

*Eleven months.
Sources: FHA yields from Federal Housing Administration; conventional yields from Federal Home Loan Bank Board, *Journal*, *Federal Reserve Bulletin*; U.S. Department of Commerce, *Construction Review*; Aaa corporate bonds are Moody's series.

the FHA rate until 1966. The extremely tight capital conditions in 1966 through 1969, together with the reluctance of investors to deal with inadequate contract yields, have placed FHA mortgages at a distinct disadvantage.

In late 1969, mortgage yields reached all-time heights. In areas particularly short of capital, yields of 9 or 10 per cent were common. This percentage is understandable because prime rate on short-term loans to the best risks was $8\frac{1}{2}$ per cent, and long-term high-grade bonds brought 9 per cent. In addition to the credit squeeze, a peculiar difficulty faced would-be borrowers—in a number of states market yields on mortgages equaled or exceeded the usury ceilings, so that new mortgage financing had to await changes in legislation.

In comparing the open-market rate on high-grade corporate bonds and on conventional mortgages, a lag in the rate of change in the latter due to the lack of a fully national flow of funds is apparent. Changes in mortgage yields appear somewhat more volatile in recent years. The spread between the annual average high-grade bond yield and the mortgage yields widens as mortgage yields rise. Although the FHA yields are now more flexible, there is aversion on the part of institutional investors to paying a price substantially different from par. Even during periods of rising effective yields, many investors are unwilling to move funds into mortgages when yields on other investments are also rising. The largest spreads between FHA and bond yields appeared in 1958, 1960, 1966, 1968, and 1969.

In spite of some development of a national market, substantial geographical differences in mortgages persist. There is still a spread between yields in the capital-surplus areas in the East and Middle Atlantic regions and in the capital-seeking West and Southwest. The spread narrows to as low as 0.25 per cent during periods of credit ease and widens to as much as 0.50 to 0.75 per cent during tight money periods. (The data in Table 11-6 do not reveal these extremes, since the national average is higher than the eastern average.) In late 1969, when the national average yield of conventional loans on new single-family homes stood at 8.3 per cent, the western rate was $8\frac{1}{2}$ to $9\frac{1}{2}$ per cent.

```
121212121212121212121212121212121212121212121212121212121212121212121212
121212121212121212121212121212121212121212121212121212121212121212121212
1212121212121212121212121   12121    121    121   1212121212121212121212
12121212121212121212121212    212   2121    121   1212121212121212121212
12121212121212121212121212121   1   12121    121   1212121212121212121212
121212121212121212121212121212     212121    121   1212121212121212121212
1212121212121212121212121212121    1212121    121   1212121212121212121212
1212121212121212121212121212121212    212121    121   1212121212121212121212
12121212121212121212121212121   1   12121    121   1212121212121212121212
12121212121212121212121212    212   2121    121   1212121212121212121212
1212121212121212121212121   12121    121    121   1212121212121212121212
121212121212121212121212121212121212121212121212121212121212121212121212
121212121212121212121212121212121212121212121212121212121212121212121212
```

Integration and the Yield Pattern

Total Sources and Uses of Funds, 1960 through 1968

Iɴ Chapters 2 through 6, the sources of funds for capital-market use were itemized for each major institution, together with their disposition in the various categories of instruments. In Chapters 7 through 11, the demand for intermediate- and long-term funds on the part of major users was set forth. In this chapter, the over-all sources and uses are collated. Four categories of sources are included that were not given separate treatment, save for the flow of their funds into various instruments: business corporations, state and local governments proper, foreign investors, and the residual—individuals and others. This last category includes bank-administered trust funds and minor institutions. Two additional uses are included in the master schedule: bank term loans to business and foreign securities acquired mainly by institutions.

Explanation of two procedures is again pertinent. First, it was noted that except for those of commercial banks, most institutional funds flow into intermediate- or long-term use. To determine commercial bank sources, data on the actual application of these funds to capital-market use were employed. Second, all maturities of Federal and Federal agency securities were considered. This procedure was based on two factors: (1) the constant transfer and arbitraging among the various maturities of these instruments, making distinction by maturity somewhat un-realistic; and (2) the lack of reliable data on the maturity composition of the investments of several institutions.

Table 12–1 combines the totals of the detailed data presented in Chapters 2 through 11 into a master array of net flows of capital-market funds for 1960 through 1968. Details on the variations of the compo-nents of the total sources and uses of capital-market funds were pre-sented in previous chapters. Recession characterized 1960. The total flow of funds into the market dropped sharply—by over $16 billions. Even though profits were off somewhat, business corporations again sold Federal securities to finance capital expenditures and to meet trade payables. Foreign investors, and especially individuals, cut their flow of funds into the market very substantially; the latter showed a nega-tive figure and a reduction of $12 billions from 1959, which reflected use of funds for debt reduction rather than new investment. The up-ward course of the total inflow of funds reappeared dramatically in 1961 with the renewal of economic expansion and continued through 1962, in spite of the stock market weakness in that year, and through 1964 and 1965. Virtually all sources increased—save for funds flowing into capital-market instruments from business corporations, which sold long-term securities in 1960 and remained out of the market until 1963.

In 1966, a year of great credit strain, major institutions reduced sharply their rate of acquisition of capital-market instruments, as the traditional flow of savings fell off substantially. That the total sources for that year equaled those of 1965 is attributable in part to the con-tinued growth of pension and retirement funds and of investment com-panies. But the major factor was the sharply increased contribution of noninstitutional suppliers of funds—federal agencies, government and foreign investors, and individuals. Their direct investments, in large part, replaced the shrinking contributions of savings institutions.

The year 1967 saw a sharp rebound in funds accumulated in institu-tions of all types, and the expansion continued well into 1968. But credit strain eventually built up and cumulated in another credit crunch in 1969, reflected in the highest yields on record in the capital market.

The data on inflow reveal a generally upward secular trend marked by instability in institutional contributions and, especially, the impact of sharply varying commercial bank investment policy.

As for uses of funds, the chief factors of instability have been the fluctuating net additions to outstanding Federal securities and mort-gages. Net changes in outstanding Federal agency securities have fol-lowed a contracyclical pattern as the agencies step up their financing in periods of pressure. As we have seen, net additions to municipal bonds fluctuate because of very special influences. Variations in net additions to corporate bonds reflect the pattern of their yields and, more im-portantly, the changing reliance by corporations on internal sources and

Table 12-1. Sources and Uses of Capital-Market Funds, 1960–1968, Billions of Dollars

	1960	1961	1962	1963	1964	1965	1966	1967	1968
Sources:									
Commercial banks	$ 3.7	$10.2	$ 9.6	$ 8.1	$ 9.6	$11.6	$ 6.1	$22.0	$20.9
Federal Reserve banks	0.7	1.5	1.9	2.8	3.4	3.8	3.5	4.8	3.8
Mutual savings banks	1.5	2.0	3.3	3.5	4.2	3.7	2.5	5.3	4.6
Savings and loan associations	7.1	9.4	10.3	13.1	11.1	9.6	4.6	9.3	9.6
Life insurance companies	4.6	5.3	5.7	6.3	7.0	7.7	6.6	7.5	7.2
Property and liability insurance companies	1.2	1.3	1.2	1.3	1.1	0.9	1.6	2.2	2.8
Corporate pension funds	3.7	3.7	3.9	4.1	4.4	5.2	5.5	6.0	6.6*
State and local government retirement funds	2.1	2.2	2.4	2.4	2.8	2.8	3.5	3.4	4.0*
Investment companies (open end)	1.2	1.4	1.5	0.8	1.1	1.6	2.0	1.1	2.4
Federal credit agencies	1.1	0.1	0.4	−0.5	−0.3	0.3	3.3	2.5	2.5
Business corporations	−5.6	0.3	0.8	1.9	−0.8	−0.9	−1.0	−1.9	1.6*
State and local governments	0.4	0.6	1.1	1.6	0.5	2.5	3.2	1.6	3.6*
Foreign investors	1.3	0.6	1.9	0.8	1.3	−0.6	−2.3	1.7	0.5*
Individuals and others	2.2	2.1	0.4	−0.2	3.7	0.4	9.9	−1.0	−0.2
Total sources	$25.2	$40.5	$44.4	$45.7	$49.1	$48.6	$48.5	$63.5	$69.9
Uses:									
U.S. government securities	$−1.8	$ 6.7	$ 8.2	$ 4.6	$ 7.0	$ 1.3	$ 2.0	$ 9.4	$11.0
Federal agency securities	—	1.1	1.7	1.5	0.4	2.1	3.8	−0.2	4.0
State and local government bonds	3.8	5.2	5.6	7.1	6.2	7.8	6.7	10.5	11.4
Bank term loans to corporations	0.1	−0.3	0.4	0.8	1.3	3.2	2.3	1.5	3.1*
Corporate bonds	5.0	5.1	4.8	5.5	6.6	8.1	11.1	15.8	14.0
Corporate stocks (all types)	1.7	2.7	0.7	−0.2	1.4	—	1.2	2.3	−0.9
Mortgages (all types)	16.0	19.5	22.3	25.7	25.8	25.7	21.2	23.8	27.1
Foreign securities	0.3	0.5	0.7	0.7	0.4	0.4	0.2	0.4	0.2*
Total uses	$25.2	$40.5	$44.4	$45.7	$49.1	$48.6	$48.5	$63.5	$69.9

*Estimated.

For sources of data, see detailed schedules in Chapters 2 through 11. Corporate bonds include term loans of life insurance companies. Some columns of sources do not add to totals because of rounding.

new stock issues. As noted in the previous chapter, the changing figures of net funds flow into mortgages reflected shifting interest-rate conditions, such as in 1966 and 1967, when other investments were relatively more attractive to some buyers, and the special factors at work in the mortgage market.

Conditions in 1968 and into 1969 reflected the continued scramble for funds on the part of individuals, governments, and corporations in the face of a much less inelastic supply, and interest rates on all capital-market credit instruments continued their upward course. Corporate stocks faced competitive yields on bonds and mortgages that equaled the historical return from combined dividends and appreciation. The efforts of the Federal administration and the monetary authorities in the summer of 1969 to stem the inflationary tide, including credit rationing by the Federal reserve, a continued high discount rate, and the extension of the income-tax surcharge, accentuated the credit crisis and encouraged record high interest yields and stock market weakness.

Capital Flows and Market Yields

The annual yield averages in Table 12-2 conceal the magnitude of interim variations. They are, however, useful in showing the relationship between the flow of funds into and out of the capital markets and the prevailing rates. The general upward drift of all series is apparent, with the exception of common stocks yields, which are affected more by special conditions than by the general supply of and demand for long-term funds. The record spread between bond and stock yields did, however, contribute substantially to the stock market weakness in 1969. The greatest volatility is found in the intermediate-term Federal rate. Mortgage yields show the least variation, reflecting the lack of a truly national competitive market.

Tight money conditions are revealed by the very high rates in 1966, 1968, and 1969 and by the excess of intermediate-term yields over long-term yields on Federal government securities in those years.

Annual changes in the bond and mortgage yields series show only a crude relationship with the changes in total supply of and demand for

Table 12-2.   Selected Capital-Market Instruments, 1960–1969

	1960	1961	1962	1963	1964	1965	1966	1967	1968	1969*
U. S. Treasury 3–5 years	4.0	3.6	3.6	3.7	4.1	4.2	5.2	5.1	5.6	6.8
U. S. Treasury long term	4.0	3.9	3.9	4.0	4.2	4.2	4.7	4.9	5.3	6.1
Aaa state and local bonds	3.3	3.3	3.0	3.1	3.1	3.2	3.7	3.7	4.2	5.4
Aaa corporate bonds	4.4	4.3	4.3	4.3	4.4	4.5	5.1	5.5	6.2	7.0
125 industrial common stocks	3.5	3.0	3.4	3.2	3.0	3.0	3.4	3.2	3.1	3.1
Conventional mortgages	6.2	6.0	5.9	5.9	5.8	5.8	6.1	6.3	6.8	7.5

*Eleven months; see previous chapters for record high yields in November.
Bond and stock yields are Moody's series. Mortgage yields are from Chapter 11.

long-term bonds funds shown in Table 12–1. In 1961, most yields declined after the strained conditions that had prevailed in the fall of 1959 and early 1960. In the Federal and corporate bond markets, the secular rise in annual yield rates was uninterrupted. Rates on municipal bonds showed more volatility and a less dramatic longer-term increase through 1965; but they exhibited the drastic conditions of general over-demand and under-supply of funds in 1966, 1968, and 1969. The effects of the enormous financing needs in all segments of the market in the latter years were discussed in previous chapters.

The question arises: Are changes in long-term yields a result or a cause of changes in the supply of and the demand for capital-market funds? Our previous discussion of the individual capital markets revealed that both possibilities are true. The question could be handled more explicitly if we were to examine in addition to data on long-term sources and uses of funds, the changing liquidity of institutional and individual suppliers. We have equated capital-market sources and uses. But we have shown neither the changes in liquid funds nor the impact of *total* funds devoted to both short- and long-term employment. Nor have we studied the shifting demand *between* short- and long-term uses. Unfortunately our short discussion does not permit such an analysis, and the reader should keep in mind the caution suggested in Chapter 1, namely, that a somewhat arbitrary segregation of the flow of long-term funds within the total investment market fails to present the total picture.

A Concluding Statement

Our study has revealed the expanding role of institutions in funneling savings into the various capital markets and the impact of their investment policies on both the primary and secondary markets for longer-term instruments. We have also shown the demands made upon the markets by individuals, businesses, and governments seeking longer-term funds for a wide variety of purposes. We have measured the combined influence of supply and demand forces on prices and yields, with special attention to the dramatic developments of the later 1960's.

The contribution of the capital markets to economic growth and the free flow of funds has increased greatly in the postwar period. The efficiency of the market structure has been enhanced by the expansion of investment banking activity, the broadening geographical range of institutional investment, the development of correspondent systems, and the improvement of secondary markets. But there are still important barriers to a really free flow of funds. Efficient capital markets require market agencies and organizations that function on a national scale, a minimum of restraints on investment policy, minimum government regulation of prices and yields, and widespread information concerning prevailing market conditions and prices so that yields can reflect the full play of supply and demand. Much progress has been made toward these goals. However, when drastic pressure for funds in the face of limited supply produces the conditions that prevailed in 1966, 1968, and 1969, the virtues of even more efficient markets, in which prices and yields reflect full national flow of and demand for funds, may conflict with national policy. Reduction in defense spending, implementation of domestic programs of great importance, and putting a brake on the inflationary spiral may require business, monetary, and fiscal controls antagonistic to unfettered markets.

References

Statistical sources are cited throughout the book. The following list is restricted to major recent works. The reader will also find most useful the May, 1964, Supplement to the *Journal of Finance*, which contains an inventory of research, both books and articles, prepared by the Exploratory Committee on Research in the Capital Markets of the National Bureau of Economic Research.

American Bankers Association, *The Commercial Banking Industry*. Englewood Cliffs, N.J.: Prentice-Hall, Inc., 1962. A monograph prepared for the Commission on Money and Credit.

American Bankers Association, Credit Policy Commission, *Term Lending by Commercial Banks*. New York, 1957.

American Institute of Banking, *Savings and Time Deposit Banking*. New York, 1968.

American Mutual Insurance Alliance *et al., Property and Casualty Insurance Companies: Their Role as Financial Intermediaries*. Englewood Cliffs, N.J.: Prentice-Hall, Inc., 1962. A monograph prepared for the Commission on Money and Credit.

Bartel, H. R., Jr., and E. T. Simpson, *Pension Funds of Multiemployer Industrial Groups, Unions, and Nonprofit Organizations*. New York: National Bureau of Economic Research, 1968.

Beckhart, B. H., ed., *Business Loans of American Commercial Banks*. New York: The Ronald Press Co., 1959.

Board of Governors of the Federal Reserve System, *Treasury–Federal Reserve Study of the Government Securities Market*. Washington, D.C.: Government Printing Office, 1960.

——, *The Federal Reserve System: Purposes and Functions*. Washington, D.C.: Government Printing Office, 1963.

——, *Flow of Funds Accounts, 1945-1967*. Washington, D.C., 1968.

Break, G. F., et al., *Federal Credit Agencies*. Englewood Cliffs, N.J.: Prentice-Hall, Inc., 1963. Research studies prepared for the Commission on Money and Credit.

Brimmer, A. F., *Life Insurance Companies in the Capital Market*. East Lansing, Mich.: Bureau of Business and Economic Research, Graduate School of Business Administration, Michigan State University, 1962.

Calvert, G. L., ed., *Fundamentals of Municipal Bonds* (5th ed.). Washington, D.C.: Investment Bankers Association of America, 1967.

Cohan, A. B., *Private Placements and Public Offerings: Market Shares Since 1935*. Chapel Hill, N.C.: University of North Carolina Press, 1961.

Colean, M. L., *Mortgage Companies: Their Place in the Financial Structure*. Englewood Cliffs, N.J.: Prentice-Hall, Inc., 1962. A monograph prepared for the Commission on Money and Credit.

Comparative Regulations of Financial Institutions. Subcommittee on Domestic Finance, House Banking and Currency Committee, U.S. Congress, 1963.

Copeland, M. A., *Trends in Government Financing*. Princeton, N.J.: Princeton University Press, 1961.

Council of Economic Advisers, *Report of the Committee on Financial Institutions to the President of the United States*. Washington, D.C.: Government Printing Office, 1963.

Cox, E. G., *Trends in the Distribution of Stock Ownership*. Philadelphia: University of Pennsylvania Press, 1963.

Crosse, H. D., *Management Policies for Commercial Banks*. Englewood Cliffs, N.J.: Prentice-Hall, Inc., 1962.

Davie, B. F., *Investment Practices of Public Employee Retirement Systems*. New York: Federal Reserve Bank of Boston, 1959.

Dawson, J. C., *A Flow-of-Funds Analysis of Savings–Investment Fluctuations in the United States*. Princeton, N.J.: Princeton University Press, 1965.

Federal National Mortgage Association, *Background and History of the Federal National Mortgage Association*. Washington, D.C., 1969.

Federal Savings Institutions. House Committee on Banking and Currency, Report No. 1642, 90th Cong., 1st sess. Washington, D.C.: Superintendent of Documents, 1967.

Fellner, William, et al., *Fiscal and Debt Management Policies*. Englewood Cliffs, N.J.: Prentice-Hall, Inc., 1963. A series of research studies prepared for the Commission on Money and Credit.

The First Boston Corporation, *Securities of the United States Government* (23rd ed.). New York: The First Boston Corporation, 1968.

Friend, Irwin, *et al.*, *The Over-the-Counter Securities Markets.* New York: McGraw-Hill Book Company, 1958.

——, *Private Capital Markets.* Englewood Cliffs, N.J.: Prentice-Hall, Inc., 1964. Research studies prepared for the Commission on Money and Credit.

——, *Investment Banking and the New Issues Market.* Cleveland: World Publishing Company, 1967.

Gaines, T. C., *Techniques of Treasury Debt Management.* New York: The Free Press, 1962.

Goldsmith, R. W., *A Study of Saving in the United States* (three volumes). Princeton, N.J.: Princeton University Press, 1955–1956.

——, *Financial Intermediaries in the American Economy Since 1900.* Princeton University Press, 1958.

——, *The Flow of Capital Funds in the Postwar Economy.* New York: Columbia University Press, 1965.

——, *Financial Institutions.* New York: Random House, Inc., 1968.

Grebler, Leo, *The Future of Thrift Institutions.* Danville, Ill.: Joint Savings and Mutual Savings Banks Exchange Groups, 1969.

Gurley, J. G., and E. E. Shaw, *Money in a Theory of Finance.* Washington, D.C.: The Brookings Institution, 1960.

Haar, C. M., *Federal Credit and Private Housing.* New York: McGraw-Hill Book Company, 1960.

Hanson, W. C., *Capital Sources and Major Investing Institutions.* New York: Simmons-Boardman Publishing Corp., 1963.

Hodgman, D. R., *Commercial Bank Loan and Investment Policy.* Champaign, Ill.: University of Illinois Bureau of Business Research, 1963.

Holland, D. M., *Private Pension Funds: Projected Growth.* New York: Columbia University Press, 1966.

Homer, Sydney, *A History of Interest Rates.* New Brunswick, N.J.: Rutgers University Press, 1963.

Horvitz, P. M., *et al.*, *Private Financial Institutions.* Englewood Cliffs, N.J.: Prentice-Hall, Inc., 1963. Research studies prepared for the Commission on Money and Credit.

Investment Company Institute, *Management Investment Companies.* Englewood Cliffs, N.J.: Prentice-Hall, Inc., 1962. A monograph prepared for the Commission on Money and Credit.

——, *The Money Managers; Professional Investment Through Mutual Funds.* New York: McGraw-Hill Book Company, 1967.

Jones, L. D., *Investment Policies of Life Insurance Companies.* Boston: Division of Research, Graduate School of Business, Harvard University, 1968.

Jones, O., and L. Grebler, *The Secondary Mortgage Market.* Los Angeles: University of California Graduate School of Business Administration, 1961.

Kendall, L. T., *The Savings and Loan Business: Its Purposes, Functions, and Economic Justification.* Englewood Cliffs, N.J.: Prentice-Hall, Inc., 1962. A monograph prepared for the Commission on Money and Credit.

Kessel, R. A., *The Cyclical Behavior of the Term Structure of Interest Rates.* New York: National Bureau of Economic Research, 1965.

Kimmel, L. H., *Share Ownership in the United States.* Washington, D.C.: The Brookings Institution, 1952.

Klaman, S. B., *The Postwar Rise of Mortgage Companies,* Occasional Paper No. 60. New York: National Bureau of Economic Research, Inc., 1959.

———, *The Postwar Residential Mortgage Market.* Princeton, N.J.: Princeton University Press, 1961.

Kuznets, Simon, *Capital in the American Economy: Its Formation and Financing.* Princeton, N.J.: Princeton University Press, 1961.

Leffler, G. L., and L. C. Farwell, *The Stock Market* (3rd ed.). New York: The Ronald Press Co., 1963.

Lent, G. E., *The Ownership of Tax-Exempt Securities, 1913-1953,* Occasional Paper 47. New York: National Bureau of Economic Research, Inc., 1955.

Levy, M. E., *Cycles in Government Securities: I. Federal Debt and Its Ownership,* New York: National Industrial Conference Board, 1963.

———, *Cycles in Government Securities: II. Determinants of Changes in Ownership.* New York: National Industrial Conference Board, 1965.

Life Insurance Association of America, *Life Insurance Companies as Financial Institutions.* Englewood Cliffs, N.J.: Prentice-Hall, Inc., 1962. A monograph prepared for the Commission on Money and Credit.

Lyon, R. A., *Investment Portfolio Management in the Commercial Bank.* New Brunswick, N.J.: Rutgers University Press, 1960.

McCahan, D., ed., *Investment of Life Insurance Funds.* Philadelphia, University of Pennsylvania Press, 1953.

McDiarmid, F. J., *Investing for a Private Institution.* New York: Life Office Management Association, 1961.

McGill, D. M., *Fundamentals of Private Pensions* (2nd ed.). Homewood, Ill.: Richard D. Irwin, Inc., 1964.

McNulty, J. E., *Decision and Influence Processes in Private Pension Plans.* Homewood, Ill.: Richard D. Irwin, Inc., 1961.

Malkiel, B. G., *The Term Structure of Interest Rates.* Princeton, N.J.: Princeton University Press, 1966.

Meiselman, D., *The Term Structure of Interest Rates.* Englewood Cliffs, N.J.: Prentice-Hall, Inc., 1962.

Money Market Instruments (2nd ed.). Cleveland: Federal Reserve Bank of Cleveland, 1965.

Mooney, G. A., *Pension and Other Employee Welfare Funds.* New York: New York State Banking Department, 1955.

Morton, J. E., *Urban Mortgage Lending: Comparative Markets and Experience.* Princeton, N.J.: Princeton University Press, 1956.

Murray, R. F., *Economic Aspects of Pensions: A Summary Report.* New York: National Bureau of Economic Research, 1968.

National Association of Mutual Savings Banks, *Mutual Savings Banks: Basic Characteristics and Role in the National Economy.* Englewood Cliffs, N.J.: Prentice-Hall, Inc., 1962. A monograph prepared for the Commission on Money and Credit.

Nelson, R. L., *The Investment Policies of Foundations.* New York: Russell Sage Foundation, 1967.

New York Stock Exchange, *Institutional Shareownership.* New York, 1964.

Pease, R. H., and L. O. Kerwood, eds., *Mortgage Banking* (2nd ed.). New York: McGraw-Hill Book Company, 1965.

Prochnow, H. V., and R. A. Foulke, *Practical Bank Credit* (2nd rev. ed.). New York: Harper & Row, Publishers, 1963.

Rabinowitz, Alan, *Municipal Bond Finance and Administration.* New York: John Wiley & Sons, Inc., 1969.

Reed, E. W., *Commercial Bank Management.* New York: Harper & Row, Publishers, 1963.

Report of the Securities and Exchange Commission of the Public Policy Implications of Investment Company Growth. Report of the Committee on Interstate and Foreign Commerce, House Report No. 2337, 89th Cong., 2d sess., December 2, 1966. Washington, D.C.: Government Printing Office, 1966.

Report of the Special Study of the Security Markets of the Securities and Exchange Commission (five parts), House Document No. 95, 88th Cong., 1st sess., Washington, D.C.: Government Printing Office, 1963.

Robbins, Sydney, *The Securities Markets: Operations and Issues.* New York: The Free Press, 1966.

Robinson, R. I., *Postwar Market for State and Local Government Securities.* Princeton, N.J.: Princeton University Press, 1960.

——, *The Management of Bank Funds* (2nd ed.). New York: McGraw-Hill Book Company, 1962.

——, *Money and Capital Markets.* New York: McGraw-Hill Book Company, 1964.

Roosa, R. V., *Federal Reserve Operations in the Money and Government Securities Market.* New York: Federal Reserve Bank of New York, 1956.

Saulnier, R. J., H. G. Halcrow, and N. H. Jacoby, *Federal Lending and Loan Insurance.* Princeton, N.J.: Princeton University Press, 1958.

Scott, I. O., Jr., *The Government Securities Market.* New York: McGraw-Hill Book Company, 1965.

Secondary Market Facilities for Conventional Mortgages. Hearings before a Subcommittee of the Committee on Banking and Currency, U.S. Senate, 88th Cong., 1st sess., September, 1963.

A Study of Federal Credit Programs. Subcommittee on Domestic Finance, Committee on Banking and Currency, House of Representatives, 88th Cong., 2d sess. Washington, D.C.: Government Printing Office, 1964.

A Study of Mortgage Credit. Subcommittee on Housing and Urban Affairs of the U.S. Senate Committee on Banking and Currency, 90th Cong., 1st sess., May 22, 1967. Washington: Government Printing Office, 1967.

A Study of Mutual Funds. Prepared for the Securities and Exchange Commission by the Wharton School of Finance and Commerce, August, 1962. Report of the Committee on Interstate and Foreign Commerce, 87th Cong., 2d sess. Washington: Government Printing Office, 1962.

Teck, Alan, *Mutual Savings Banks and Savings and Loan Associations: Aspects of Growth.* New York: Columbia University Press, 1968.

Walter, J. E., *The Role of Regional Security Exchanges.* Berkeley, Calif.: University of California Press, 1957.

——, *The Investment Process as Characterized by Leading Life Insurance Companies.* Boston: Division of Research, Graduate School of Business, Harvard University, 1962.

Waterman, M. H., *Investment Banking Functions.* Ann Arbor, Mich.: Bureau of Business Research, University of Michigan, 1958.

Welfing, Weldon, *Bank Investments.* New York: American Bankers Association, American Institute of Banking, 1963.

——, *Mutual Savings Banks: The Evolution of a Financial Intermediary.* Cleveland: Press of Case Western Reserve University, 1968.

Index